TABLE OF CONTENTS

Top 20 Test Taking Tips

1. Carefully follow all the test registration procedures
2. Know the test directions, duration, topics, question types, how many questions
3. Setup a flexible study schedule at least 3-4 weeks before test day
4. Study during the time of day you are most alert, relaxed, and stress free
5. Maximize your learning style; visual learner use visual study aids, auditory learner use auditory study aids
6. Focus on your weakest knowledge base
7. Find a study partner to review with and help clarify questions
8. Practice, practice, practice
9. Get a good night's sleep; don't try to cram the night before the test
10. Eat a well balanced meal
11. Know the exact physical location of the testing site; drive the route to the site prior to test day
12. Bring a set of ear plugs; the testing center could be noisy
13. Wear comfortable, loose fitting, layered clothing to the testing center; prepare for it to be either cold or hot during the test
14. Bring at least 2 current forms of ID to the testing center
15. Arrive to the test early; be prepared to wait and be patient
16. Eliminate the obviously wrong answer choices, then guess the first remaining choice
17. Pace yourself; don't rush, but keep working and move on if you get stuck
18. Maintain a positive attitude even if the test is going poorly
19. Keep your first answer unless you are positive it is wrong
20. Check your work, don't make a careless mistake

Historical Concepts and Skills

Graphic Format

The type of information being conveyed guides the choice of format. Textual information and numeric information must be displayed with different techniques. Text-only information may be most easily summarized in a diagram or a timeline. If text includes numeric information, it may be converted into a chart that shows the size of groups, connects ideas in a table or graphic, or shows information in a hybridized format. Ideas or opinions can be effectively conveyed in political cartoons. Numeric information is often most helpfully presented in tables or graphs. When information will be referred to and looked up again and again, tables are often most helpful for the reader. When the trends in the numeric information are more important than the numbers themselves, graphs are often the best choice. Information that is linked to the land and has a spatial component is best conveyed using maps.

Reference Materials

Encyclopedias are ideal for getting background information on a topic. They provide an overview of the topic, and link it to other concepts that can provide additional keywords, information, or subjects. They can help students narrow their topic by showing the sub-topics within the overall topic, and by relating it to other topics. Encyclopedias are often more useful than the Internet because they provide a clearly organized, concise overview of material.

Bibliographies are bound collections of references to periodicals and books, organized by topic. Students can begin researching more efficiently after they identify a topic, look it up in a bibliography, and look up the references listed there. This provides a branching network of information a student can follow. A pitfall of bibliographies is that when in textbooks or other journal articles, the references in them are chosen to support the author's point of view, and so may be limited in scope.

Almanacs are volumes of facts published annually. They provide numerical information on just about every topic, and are organized by subject or geographic region. They are often helpful for supporting arguments made using other resources, and do not provide any interpretation of their own.

Electronic resources are often the quickest, most convenient way to get background information on a topic. One of the particular strengths of electronic resources is that they can also provide primary-source multimedia video, audio, or other visual information on a topic that would not be accessible in print. Information available on the Internet is not often carefully screened for accuracy or for bias, so choosing the source of electronic information is often very important. Electronic encyclopedias can provide excellent overview information, but publicly edited resources like Wikipedia are open to error, rapid change, incompleteness, or bias. Students should be made aware of the different types and reliabilities of electronic resources, and they should be taught how to distinguish between them. Electronic resources can often be too detailed and overwhelm students with irrelevant information.

Periodicals provide current information on social science events, but they too must be screened for bias. Some amount of identifiable bias can actually be an important source of information, because it indicates prevailing culture and standards. Periodicals generally have tighter editorial standards than electronic resources, so completeness and overt errors are not usually as problematic. Periodicals can also provide primary-source information with interviews and photographs.

Resources

Primary resources provide information about an event from the perspective of people who were present at the event. They might be letters, autobiographies, interviews, speeches, artworks, or anything created by people with first-hand experience. Primary resources are valuable because they provide not only facts about the event, but also information about the surrounding circumstances; for example, a letter might provide commentary about how a political speech was received. The Internet is a source of primary information, but care must be taken to evaluate the perspective of the website providing that information. Websites hosted by individuals or special-interest organizations are more likely to be biased than those hosted by public organizations, governments, educational institutions, or news associations.

Secondary resources provide information about an event, but were not written at the time the event occurred. They draw information from primary sources. Because secondary sources were written later, they have the added advantage of historical perspective, multiple points of view, or resultant outcomes. Newsmagazines that write about an event even a week after it occurred count as secondary sources. Secondary sources tend to analyze events more effectively or thoroughly than primary sources.

Research Paper

The first step of writing a research paper involves narrowing down on a topic. The student should first read background information to identify areas that are interesting or need further study and that the student does not have a strong opinion about. The research question should be identified, and the student should refer to general sources that can point to more specific information. When he begins to take notes, his information must be organized with a clear system to identify the source. Any information from outside sources must be acknowledged with footnotes or a bibliography. To gain more specific information about his topic, the student can then research bibliographies of the general sources to narrow down on information pertinent to his topic. He should draft a thesis statement that summarizes the main point of the research. This should lead to a working outline that incorporates all the ideas needed to support the main point in a logical order. A rough draft should incorporate the results of the research in the outlined order, with all citations clearly inserted. The paper should then be edited for clarity, style, flow, and content.

Hypotheses

Formulating research questions or hypotheses is the process of finding questions to answer that have not yet been asked. The first step in the process is reading background information. Knowing about a general topic and reading about how other people have addressed it helps identify areas that are well understood. Areas that are not as well understood may either be lightly addressed in the available literature, or distinctly identified as a topic that is not well understood and deserves further study. Research questions or hypotheses may address such an unknown aspect, or they may focus on drawing parallels between similar, well-researched topics that have not been connected before. Students usually need practice in developing research questions that are of the appropriate scope so that they will find enough information to answer the question, yet not so much that they become overwhelmed. Hypotheses tend to be more specific than research questions.

Main Ideas

Main ideas in a paragraph are often found in the topic sentence, which is usually the first or second sentence in the paragraph. Every following sentence in the paragraph should relate to that initial information. Sometimes, the first or second sentence doesn't obviously set up the main idea. When that happens, each sentence in the paragraph should be read carefully to find the common theme between them all. This common theme is the main idea of the paragraph.

Main ideas in an entire document can be found by analyzing the structure of the document. Frequently, the document begins with an introductory paragraph or abstract that will summarize the main ideas. Each paragraph often discusses one of the main ideas and contributes to the overall goal of the document. Some documents are divided up into chapters or sections, each of which discusses a main idea. The way that main ideas are described in a document (either in sentences, paragraphs, or chapters) depends on the length of the document.

Artifacts

Artifacts, or everyday objects used by previous cultures, are useful for understanding life in those cultures. Students should first discover, or be provided with, a description of the item. This description should tell during what period the artifact was used and what culture used it. From that description and/or from examination of the artifact, students should be able to discuss what the artifact is, what it is made of, its potential uses, and the people who likely used it. They should then be able to draw conclusions from all these pieces of evidence about life in that culture. For example, analysis of coins from an early American archaeological site might show that settlers brought coins with them, or that some classes of residents were wealthy, or that trade occurred with many different nations. The interpretation will vary depending on the circumstances surrounding the artifact. Students should consider these circumstances when drawing conclusions.

Cause and Effect

Cause-and-effect relationships are simply linkages between an event that happened (the effect) because of some other event (the cause). Effects are always chronologically ordered after causes. Effects can be found by asking why something happened, or looking for information following words like so, consequently, since, because, therefore, this led to, as a result, and thus. Causes can be found by asking what happened.

Comparing similarities and differences involves mentally setting two concepts next to each other and then listing the ways they are the same and the ways they are different. The level of comparison varies by student level; for example, younger students may compare the physical characteristics of two animals while older students compare the themes of a book. Similarity/difference comparisons can be done by listing written descriptions in a point-by-point approach, or they can be done in several graphic ways. Venn diagrams are commonly used to organize information, showing non-overlapping clouds filled with information about the different characteristics of A and B, and the overlapping area shows ways in which A and B are the same. Idea maps using arrows and bubbles can also be developed to show these differences.

Organizing Information

To organize information chronologically, each piece of information must be associated with a time or a date. Events are ordered according to the time or date at which they happened. In social sciences, chronological organization is the most straightforward way to arrange information, because it relies on a uniform, fixed scale – the passage of time. Information can also be organized based on any of the "who, what, when, where, why?" principles.

Analyzing the sequence of chronological events involves not only examining the event itself, but the preceding and following events. This can put the event in question into perspective, showing how a certain thing might have happened based on preceding history. One large disadvantage of chronological organization is that it may not highlight important events clearly relative to less important events. Determining the relative importance of events depends more strongly on interpreting their relationships to neighboring events.

Before information is sought, a list of guiding questions should be developed to help determine whether information found is adequate, relevant, and consistent. These questions should be based on the research goals, which should be laid out in an outline or concept map. For example, a student writing a report on Navajo social structure might begin with questions concerning the general lifestyle and location of Navajos, and follow with questions about how Navajo society was organized. While researching his questions, he will come up with pieces of information. This information can be compared to his research questions to determine whether it is relevant to his report. Information from several sources should be compared to determine whether information is consistent. Information that is adequate helps answer specific questions that are part of the research goals. Inadequate information for this particular student might be a statement such as "Navajos had a strong societal structure," because the student is probably seeking more specific information.

Fact vs. Opinion

Students easily recognize that facts are true statements that everyone agrees on, such as an object's name or a statement about a historical event. Students also recognize that opinions vary about matters of taste, such as preferences in food or music, that rely on people's interpretation of facts. Simple examples are easy to spot. Fact-based passages include certainty-grounded words like is, did, or saw. On the other hand, passages containing opinions often include words that indicate possibility rather than certainty, such as would, should or believe. First-person verbs also indicate opinions, showing that one person is talking about his experience.

Less clear are examples found in higher-level texts. For example, primary-source accounts of a Civil War battle might include facts ("X battle was fought today") and also opinions ("Union soldiers are not as brave as Confederate soldiers") that are not clearly written as such ("I believe Union soldiers..."). At the same time as students learn to interpret sources critically (Was the battle account written by a Southerner?), they should practice sifting fact from these types of opinion. Other examples where fact and opinion blend together are self-authored internet websites.

Drawing Conclusions

Students reading about a topic will encounter different facts and opinions that contribute to their overall impression of the material. The student can critically examine the material by thinking about what facts have been included, how they have been presented, what they show, what they relate to outside the written material, and what the author's conclusion is. Students may agree or disagree with the author's conclusion, based on the student's interpretation of the facts the author presented. When working on a research project, a student's research questions will help him gather details that will enable him to draw a conclusion about the research material.

Generalizations are blanket statements that apply to a wide number of examples. They are similar to conclusions, but do not have to summarize the information as completely as conclusions. Generalizations in reading material may be flagged by words such as all, most, none, many, several, sometimes, often, never, overall, or in general. Generalizations are often followed by supporting information consisting of a list of facts. Generalizations can refer to facts or the author's opinions, and they provide a valuable summary of the text overall.

Map Interpretation

The map legend is an area that provides interpretation information such as the key, the scale, and how to interpret the map. The key is the area that defines symbols, abbreviations, and color schemes used on the map. Any feature identified on the map should be defined in the key. The scale is a feature of the map legend that tells how distance on the map relates to distance on the ground. It can either be presented mathematically in a ratio or visually with a line segment. For example, it could say that one inch on the map equals one foot on the ground, or it could show a line segment and tell how much distance on the map the line symbolizes. Latitude and longitude are often shown on maps to relate their area to the world. Latitude shows how far a location is north or south from the earth's equator, and longitude shows how far a location is east or west from the earth's prime meridian. Latitude runs from 90 N (North Pole) – 0 (equator) – 90 S (South Pole), and longitude runs 180 E (international date line) – 0 (prime meridian) – 180 W (international date line).

Cartographic Distortion

Cartographic distortion is the distortion caused by projecting a three-dimensional structure, in this case the surface of the earth, onto the two-dimensional surface of a map. Numerous map projections have been developed to minimize distortion, but the only way to eliminate distortion completely is to render the earth in three dimensions. Most map projections

- 9 -

have minimal distortion in some location, usually the center, and the distortion becomes greater close to the edges of the map. Some map projections try to compromise and distribute the distortion more evenly across the map. Different categories of maps preserve, or do not distort, different features. Maps that preserve directions accurately are azimuthal, and maps that preserve shapes properly are conformal. Area-preserving maps are called equal-area maps, and maps that preserve distance are called distance-preserving. Maps that preserve the shortest routes are gnomonic projections.

Map Projections

Globe: Earth's features are shown on a sphere. No distortion of distances, directions, or areas occurs.
Mercator: projects Earth's features onto a cylinder wrapped around a globe. Generates a rectangular map that is not distorted at the equator but is greatly distorted near the poles. Lines of latitude and longitude form a square grid.
Robinson: projects Earth's features onto an oval-looking map. Areas near the poles are truer to size than in the Mercator. Some distortion affects every point.
Orthographic: Earth's features are shown on a circle, which is tangent to the globe at any point chosen by the mapmaker. Generates a circular, 3D-appearing map similar to how Earth is seen from space.
Conic maps: A family of maps drawn by projecting the globe's features onto a cone set onto the globe. Some distortion affects most points.
Polar maps: A circle onto which the land around the poles has been projected. Provides much less distortion of Antarctica and the land around the North Pole than other map types.

Comparing Maps

Maps of the same place from different time periods can often be initially aligned by geographic features. Political and land-use boundaries are most likely to change between time periods, whereas locations of waterways and geologic features such as mountains are relatively constant. Once geographic features have been used to align maps, they can be compared side-by-side to examine the changing locations of human settlement, smaller waterways, etc. This kind of map interpretation, at the smallest scale, provides information about how small groups of humans interact with their environment. For example, such analysis might show that major cities began around ports, and then moved inland as modes of transportation, like railroads and cars, became more common. Lands that were initially used for agriculture might become incorporated into a nearby city as the population grows. This kind of map analysis can also show the evolution of the socio-economics of an area, providing information about the relative importance of economic activities (manufacturing, agriculture or trade) and even the commuting behavior of workers.

Maps can provide a great deal of information about an area by showing specific locations where certain types of settlement, land use, or population growth occurred. Datasets and texts can provide more specific information about events that can be hypothesized from maps. This specific information may provide dates of significant events (for example, the date of a fire that gutted a downtown region, forcing suburban development) or important numerical data (e.g., population growth by year). Written datasets and texts enable map interpretation to become concrete and allow observed trends to be linked with specific causes ("Real estate prices rose in 2004, causing middle-class citizens to move northwest of the city"). Without specific information from additional sources, inferences drawn from maps cannot be put in context and interpreted in more than a vague way.

Map legends will provide information about the types of natural, political, or cultural features on a map. Some maps show only one of these three features. Natural features such as waterways, wetlands, beaches, deserts, mountains, highlands and plains can be compared between regions by type, number, distribution, or any other physical characteristic. Political features such as state and county divisions or roads and railroads can be compared numerically, but examining their geographic distribution may be more informative. This provides information on settlement density and population. In addition, road and railroad density may show regions of intense urbanization, agricultural regions, or industrial centers. Cultural features may include roads and railroads, but might also include historic areas, museums, archaeological digs, early settlements and even campgrounds. Comparing and contrasting the number, distribution, and types of these features may provide information on the history of an area, the duration of settlement of an area, or the current use of the area (for example, many museums are found in current-day cultural centers).

Interpreting Graphs and Diagrams

Graphs are similar to charts, except that they graphically show numeric information on both axes. For example, a graph might show population through the years, with years on the X-axis and population on the Y-axis. One advantage of graphs is that population during the time in between censuses can be estimated by locating that point on the graph. Each axis should be labeled to allow the information to be interpreted correctly, and the graph should have an informative title.

Diagrams are usually drawings that show the progression of events. The drawings can be fairly schematic, as in a flow chart, or they can be quite detailed, as in a depiction of scenes from a battle. Diagrams usually have arrows connecting the events or boxes shown. Each event or box should be labeled to show what it represents. Diagrams are interpreted by following the progression along the arrows through all events.

Interpreting Charts and Tables

Charts used in social science are a visual representation of data. They combine graphic and textual elements to convey information in a concise format. Often, charts divide the space up in blocks, which are filled with text and/or pictures to convey a point. Charts are often organized in tabular form, where blocks below a heading all have information in common. Charts also divide information into conceptual, non-numeric groups (for example, "favorite color"), which are then plotted against a numerical axis (e.g., "number of students"). Charts should be labeled in such a way that a reader can locate a point on the chart and then consult the surrounding axes or table headings to understand how it compares to other points.

Tables are a type of chart that divides textual information into rows and columns. Each row and column represents a characteristic of the information. For example, a table might be used to convey demographic information. The first column would provide "year," and the second would provide "population." Reading across the rows, one could see that in the year 1966, the population of Middletown was 53,847. Tracking the columns would show how frequently the population was counted.

Political Cartoons

Political cartoons are drawings that memorably convey an opinion. These opinions may be supportive or critical, and may summarize a series of events or pose a fictional situation that summarizes an attitude. Political cartoons are therefore secondary sources of information that provide social and cultural context about events. Political cartoons may have captions that help describe the action or put it in context. They may also have dialogue, labels, or other recognizable cultural symbols. For example, Uncle Sam frequently appears in political cartoons to represent the United States Government. Political cartoons frequently employ caricature to call attention to a situation or a person. The nature of the caricature helps show the cartoonist's attitude toward the issue being portrayed. Every element of the cartoon is included to support the artist's point, and should be considered in the cartoon's interpretation. When interpreting political cartoons, students should examine what issue is being discussed, what elements the artist chose to support his or her point, and what the message is. Considering who might agree or disagree with the cartoon is also helpful in determining the message of the cartoon.

Timelines

Timelines are used to show the relationships between people, places, and events. They are ordered chronologically, and usually are shown left-to-right or top-to-bottom. Each event on the timeline is associated with a date, which determines its location on the timeline. On electronic resources, timelines often contain hyperlinks associated with each event. Clicking on the event's hyperlink will open a page with more information about the event. Cause-and-effect relationships can be observed on timelines, which often show a key event and then resulting events following in close succession. These can be helpful for showing the order of events in time or the relationships between similar events. They help make the passage of time a concrete concept, and show that large periods pass between some events, and other events cluster very closely.

World History to 1450 A.D.

Prehistory

Prehistory is the period of human history before writing was developed. The three major periods of prehistory are:

Lower Paleolithic—Humans used crude tools.

Upper Paleolithic—Humans began to develop a wider variety of tools. These tools were better made and more specialized. They also began to wear clothes, organize in groups with definite social structures, and to practice art. Most lived in caves during this time period.

Neolithic—Social structures became even more complex, including growth of a sense of family and the ideas of religion and government. Humans learned to domesticate animals and produce crops, build houses, start fires with friction tools, and to knit, spin and weave.

Anthropology

Anthropology is the study of human culture. Anthropologists study groups of humans, how they relate to each other, and the similarities and differences between these different groups and cultures. Anthropological research takes two approaches: cross-cultural research and comparative research. Most anthropologists work by living among different cultures and participating in those cultures in order to learn about them.

There are three major divisions within anthropology:

Biological and cultural anthropology

Archaeology

Linguistics

Archeology

Archeology studies past human cultures by evaluating what they leave behind. This can include bones, buildings, art, tools, pottery, graves, and even trash. Archeologists maintain detailed notes and records of their findings and use special tools to evaluate what they find. Photographs, notes, maps, artifacts, and surveys of the area can all contribute to evaluation of an archeological site. By studying all these elements of numerous archeological sites, scientists have been able to theorize that humans or near-humans have existed for about 600,000 years. Before that, more primitive humans are believed to have appeared about one million years ago. These humans eventually developed into Cro-Magnon man, and then Homo sapiens, or modern man.

Human Development

Human development has been divided into several phases:

Lower Paleolithic or Old Stone Age, about one million years ago—early humans used tools like needles, hatchets, awls, and cutting tools.

Upper Paleolithic or New Stone Age, 6,000-8,000 BCE—also known as the Neolithic, textiles and pottery are developed. Humans of this era discovered the wheel, began to practice agriculture, made polished tools, and had some domesticated animals.

Bronze Age, 3,000 BCE—metals are discovered and the first civilizations emerge as humans become more technologically advanced.
Iron Age, 1,200-1,000 BCE—metal tools replace stone tools as humans develop knowledge of smelting.

Civilizations

Civilizations are defined as having the following characteristics:
Use of metal to make weapons and tools
Written language
A defined territorial state
A calendar

The earliest civilizations developed in river valleys where reliable, fertile land was easily found, including:
Nile River valley in Egypt
Mesopotamia
Indus River
Hwang Ho in China

The very earliest civilizations developed in the Tigris-Euphrates valley in Mesopotamia, which is now part of Iraq, and in Egypt's Nile valley. These civilizations arose between 4,000 and 3,000 BCE. The area where these civilizations grew is known as the Fertile Crescent. There, geography and the availability of water made large-scale human habitation possible.

<u>Importance of rivers and water</u>
The earliest civilizations are also referred to as fluvial civilizations because they were founded near rivers. Rivers and the water they provide were vital to these early groupings, offering:
Water for drinking and cultivating crops
A gathering place for wild animals that could be hunted
Easily available water for domesticated animals
Rich soil deposits as a result of regular flooding

Irrigation techniques helped direct water where it was most needed, to sustain herds of domestic animals and to nourish crops of increasing size and quality.

Fertile Crescent

James Breasted, an archeologist from the University of Chicago, coined the term Fertile Crescent to describe the area in the Near East where the earliest civilizations arose. The region includes modern day Iraq, Syria, Lebanon, Israel/Palestine and Jordan. It is bordered on the south by the Arabian Desert, the west by the Mediterranean Sea, and to the north and east by the Taurus and Zagros Mountains respectively. This area not only provided the raw materials for the development of increasingly advanced civilizations, but also saw waves of migration and invasion, leading to the earliest wars and genocides as groups conquered and absorbed each other's cultures and inhabitants.

Egyptian, Sumerian, Babylonian and Assyrian Cultures

The Egyptians were one of the most advanced ancient cultures, having developed construction methods to build the great pyramids, as well as a form of writing known as hieroglyphics. Their religion was highly developed and complex, and included advanced techniques for the preservation of bodies after death. They also made paper by processing papyrus, a plant commonly found along the Nile, invented the decimal system, devised a solar calendar, and advanced overall knowledge of arithmetic and geometry.

The Sumerians were the first to invent the wheel, and also brought irrigation systems into use. Their cuneiform writing was simpler than Egyptian hieroglyphs, and they developed the timekeeping system we still use today.

The Babylonians are best known for the Code of Hammurabi, an advanced law code.

The Assyrians developed horse-drawn chariots and an organized military.

Hebrew, Persian, Minoan, and Mycenaean Cultures

The Hebrew or ancient Israelite culture developed the monotheistic religion that eventually developed into modern Judaism and Christianity.

The Persians were conquerors, but those they conquered were allowed to keep their own laws, customs, and religious traditions rather than being forced to accept those of their conquerors. They also developed an alphabet and practicing Zoroastrianism, Mithraism and Gnosticism, religions that have influenced modern religious practice.

The Minoans used a syllabic writing system and built large, colorful palaces. These ornate buildings included sewage systems, running water, bathtubs, and even flush toilets. Their script, known as Linear Script A, has yet to be deciphered.

The Mycenaeans practiced a religion that grew into the Greek pantheon, worshipping Zeus and other Olympian gods. They developed Linear Script B, a writing system used to write an ancient form of classical Greek.

Phoenicians and Early Culture in India and Ancient China

Skilled seafarers and navigators, the Phoenicians used the stars to navigate their ships at night. They developed a purple dye that was in great demand in the ancient world, and worked with glass and metals. They also devised their own phonetic alphabet, using symbols to represent individual sounds rather than whole words or syllables.

In the Indus Valley, an urban civilization arose in what is now India. These ancient humans developed the concept of zero in mathematics, practiced an early form of the Hindu religion, and developed a caste system which is still prevalent in India today. Archeologists are still uncovering information about this highly developed ancient civilization.

In ancient China, human civilization developed along the Yangtze River, starting as long as 500,000 years ago. These people produced silk, grew millet, and made pottery, including Longshan black pottery.

Civilizations of Mesopotamia

The major civilizations of Mesopotamia, in what is now called the Middle East, were:
Sumerians
Amorites
Hittites
Assyrians

Chaldeans
Persians

These cultures controlled different areas of Mesopotamia during various time periods, but were similar in that they were autocratic. This meant a single ruler served as the head of the government and often, the main religious ruler, as well. These, often tyrannical, militaristic leaders, controlled all aspects of life, including law, trade, and religious activity. Portions of the legacies of these civilizations remain in cultures today. These include mythologies, religious systems, mathematical innovations and even elements of various languages.

Sumer

Sumer, located in the southern part of Mesopotamia, consisted of a dozen city-states. Each city-state had its own gods, and the leader of each city-state also served as the high priest. Cultural legacies of Sumer include:
The invention of writing
Invention of the wheel
The first library—established in Assyria by Ashurbanipal
The Hanging Gardens of Babylon—one of the Seven Wonders of the Ancient World
First written laws—Ur-Nammu's Codes and the Codes of Hammurabi
The *Epic of Gilgamesh*—the first epic story in history

Kushite Culture

Kush, or Cush, was located south of ancient Egypt, and the earliest existing records of this civilization were found in Egyptian texts. At one time, Kush was the largest empire on the Nile River, surpassing even Egypt.

In Neolithic times, Kushites lived in villages, with buildings made of mud bricks. They were settled rather than nomadic, and practiced hunting and fishing, cultivated grain, and also herded cattle. Kerma, the capitol, was a major center of trade.

Kush determined leadership through matrilineal descent of their kings, as did Egypt. Their heads of state, the Kandake or Kentake, were female. Their polytheistic religion included the primary Egyptian gods as well as regional gods, including a lion god, which is commonly found in African cultures.

Archeological evidence indicates the Kushites were a mix of Mediterranean and Negroid peoples. Kush was conquered by Nubia in 800 BCE.

Minoan Civilization

The Minoans lived on the island of Crete, just off the coast of Greece. This civilization reigned from 2700 to 1450 BCE. The Minoans developed writing systems known to linguists as Linear A and Linear B. Linear A has not yet been translated; Linear B evolved into classical Greek script. "Minoans" is not the name they used for themselves, but is instead a variation on the name of King Minos, a king in Greek mythology believed by some to have been a denizen of Crete. The Minoan civilization subsisted on trade, and their way of life was often disrupted by earthquakes and volcanoes. Much is still unknown about the Minoans, and archeologists continue to study their architecture and archeological remains. The Minoan culture eventually fell to Greek invaders and was supplanted by the Mycenaean civilization.

Ancient Indian Civilization Influences

The civilizations of ancient India gave rise to both Hinduism and Buddhism, major world religions that have found their way to countries far away from their place of origin. Practices such as yoga, increasingly popular in the West, can trace their roots to these earliest Indian civilizations. Literature from ancient India includes the *Mahabharata* containing the *Bhagavad Gita,* the *Ramayana*, *Arthashastra*, and the *Vedas*, a collection of sacred texts. Indo-European languages, including English, find their beginnings in these ancient cultures. Ancient Indo-Aryan languages such as Sanskrit are still used in some formal Hindu practices. Yoga poses are still formally referred to by Sanskrit names.

Earliest Chinese Civilizations

Many historians believe Chinese civilization is the oldest uninterrupted civilization in the world. The Neolithic age in China goes back 10,000 years, with agriculture in China beginning as early as 7,000 years ago. Their system of writing dates to 1,500 BCE. The Yellow River served as the center for the earliest Chinese settlements. In Ningxia, in northwest China, there are carvings on cliffs that date back to the Paleolithic Period, at least 6,000 years ago, indicating the extreme antiquity of Chinese culture. Literature from ancient China includes works by Confucius, *Analects*, the *Tao Te Ching*, and a variety of poetry.

Ancient American Cultures

Less is known of ancient American civilizations since less was left behind. Those we know something of include:
The Norte Chico civilization in Peru, an agricultural society of 20 individual communities, that existed over 5,000 years ago. This culture is also known as Caral-Supe, and is the oldest known civilization in the Americas.
The Anasazi, or Ancient Pueblo People, in what is now the southwestern United States. Emerging about 1200 BCE, the Anasazi built complex adobe dwellings, and were the forerunners of later Pueblo Indian cultures.
The Maya emerged in southern Mexico and northern Central America as early as 2,600 BCE. They developed a written language and a complex calendar.

Mycenaean Civilization

The Mycenaean civilization was the first major civilization in Europe. In contrast to the Minoans, whom they displaced, the Mycenaeans relied more on conquest than on trade. Mycenaean states included Sparta, Metropolis and Corinth. The history of this civilization, including the Trojan War, was recorded by the Greek poet, Homer. His work was largely considered mythical until archeologists discovered evidence of the city of Troy in Hisarlik, Turkey. Archeologists continue to add to the body of information about this ancient culture, translating documents written in Linear B, a script derived from the Minoan Linear A. It is theorized that the Mycenaean civilization was eventually destroyed in either a Dorian invasion or an attack by Greek invaders from the north. This theory has not been proven, nor is it certain who the invaders might have been

Dorian Invasion

A Dorian invasion does not refer to an invasion by a particular group of people, but rather is a hypothetical theory to explain the end of the Mycenaean civilization and the growth of classical Greece. Ancient tradition refers to these events as "the return of the Heracleidae," or the sons (descendents) of Hercules. Archeologists and historians still do not know exactly who conquered the Mycenaean, but it is believed to have occurred around 1200 BCE, contemporaneous with the destruction of the Hittite civilization in what is now modern Turkey. The Hittites speak of an attack by people of the Aegean Sea, or the "Sea People." Only Athens was left intact.

Spartans and Athenians

Both powerful city-states, the Spartans and the Athenians nurtured contrasting cultures. The Spartans, located in Peloponnesus, were ruled by an oligarchic military state. They practiced farming, disallowed trade for Spartan citizens, and valued military arts and strict discipline. They emerged as the strongest military force in the area, and maintained this status for many years. In one memorable encounter, a small group of Spartans held off a huge army of Persians at Thermopylae.

The Athenians were centered in Attica, where there was little land available for farming. Like the Spartans, they descended from invaders who spoke Greek. Their government was very different from Sparta's; it was in Athens that democracy was created by Cleisthenes of Athens in 510 BCE. Athenians excelled in art, theater, architecture, and philosophy.

Athens and Sparta fought each other in the Peloponnesian War, 431-404 BCE.

Ancient Greece Contributions

Ancient Greece made numerous major contributions to cultural development, including:
Theater—Aristophanes and other Greek playwrights laid the groundwork for modern theatrical performance.
Alphabet—the Greek alphabet, derived from the Phoenician alphabet, developed into the Roman alphabet, and then into our modern-day alphabet.
Geometry—Pythagoras and Euclid pioneered much of the system of geometry still taught today. Archimedes made various mathematical discoveries, including the value of pi.

Historical writing—much of ancient history doubles as mythology or religious texts. Herodotus and Thucydides made use of research and interpretation to record historical events.

Philosophy—Socrates, Plato, and Aristotle served as the fathers of Western philosophy. Their work is still required reading for philosophy students.

Alexander the Great

Born to Philip II of Macedon and tutored by Aristotle, Alexander the Great is considered one of the greatest conquerors in history. He conquered Egypt, the Achaemenid/Persian Empire, a powerful empire founded by Cyrus the Great that spanned three continents, and he traveled as far as India and the Iberian Peninsula. Though Alexander died at the early age of 32, his conquering efforts spread Greek culture into the east. This cultural diffusion left a greater mark on history than did his empire, which fell apart due to internal conflict not long after his death. Trade between the East and West increased, as did an exchange of ideas and beliefs that influenced both regions greatly. The Hellenistic traditions his conquest spread were prevalent in Byzantine culture until as late as the 15th century.

Hittite Empire

The Hittites were centered in what is now Turkey, but their empire extended into Palestine and Syria. They conquered the Babylonian civilization, but adopted their religion and their system of laws. Overall, the Hittites tended to tolerate other religions, unlike many other contemporary cultures, and absorbed foreign gods into their own belief systems rather than forcing their religion onto peoples they conquered. The Hittite Empire reached its peak in 1600-1200 BCE. After a war with Egypt, which weakened them severely, they were eventually conquered by the Assyrians in 700 BCE.

Persian Wars

The Persian Empire, ruled by Cyrus the Great, encompassed an area from the Black Sea to Afghanistan, and beyond into Central Asia. After the death of Cyrus, Darius became king in 522 BCE. The empire reached its zenith during his reign.

From 499-448 BCE, the Greeks and Persians fought in the Persian Wars. Battles of the Persian Wars included:

The Battle of Marathon, in which heavily outnumbered Greek forces managed to achieve victory.

The Battle of Thermopylae, in which a small band of Spartans held off a throng of Persian troops for several days.

The Battle of Salamis, a naval battle that again saw outnumbered Greeks achieving victory.

The Battle of Plataea, another Greek victory, but one in which they outnumbered the Persians.

The Persian Wars did not see the end of the Persian Empire, but discouraged additional attempts to invade Greece.

Maurya Empire

The Maurya Empire was a large, powerful empire established in India. It was one of the largest ever to rule in the Indian subcontinent, and existed from 322 to 185 BCE, ruled by

Chandragupta after the withdrawal from India of Alexander the Great. The Maurya Empire was highly developed, including a standardized economic system, waterworks, and private corporations. Trade to the Greeks and others became common, with goods including silk, exotic foods, and spices. Religious development included the rise of Buddhism and Jainism. The laws of the Maurya Empire protected not only civil and social rights of the citizens, but also protected animals, establishing protected zones for economically important creatures such as elephants, lions and tigers. This period of time in Indian history was largely peaceful due to the strong Buddhist beliefs of many of its leaders. The empire finally fell after a succession of weak leaders, and was taken over by Demetrius, a Greco-Bactrian king who took advantage of this lapse in leadership to conquer southern Afghanistan and Pakistan around 180 BCE.

Chinese Empires

In China, history was divided into a series of dynasties. The most famous of these, the Han Dynasty, existed from 206 BCE to 220 CE. Accomplishments of the Chinese Empires included:
Building the Great Wall of China
Numerous inventions, including paper, paper money, printing, and gunpowder
High level of artistic development
Silk production

The Chinese Empires were comparable to Rome as far as their artistic and intellectual accomplishments, as well as the size and scope of their influence.

Roman Empire and Republic

Rome began humbly, in a single town that grew out of Etruscan settlements and traditions, founded, according to legend, by twin brothers Romulus and Remus, who were raised by wolves. Romulus killed Remus, and from his legacy grew Rome. A thousand years later, the Roman Empire covered a significant portion of the known world, from what is now Scotland, across Europe, and into the Middle East. Hellenization, or the spread of Greek culture throughout the world, served as an inspiration and a model for the spread of Roman culture. Rome brought in belief systems of conquered peoples as well as their technological and scientific accomplishments, melding the disparate parts into a Roman core. Rome's overall government was autocratic, but local officials came from the provinces where they lived. This limited administrative system was probably a major factor in the long life of the empire.

Byzantine Empire

In the early fourth century, the Roman Empire split, with the eastern portion becoming the Eastern Empire, or the Byzantine Empire. In 330 CE, Constantine founded the city of Constantinople, which became the center of the Byzantine Empire. Its major influences came from Mesopotamia and Persia, in contrast to the Western Empire, which maintained traditions more closely linked to Greece and Carthage. Byzantium's position gave it an advantage over invaders from the west and the east, as well as control over trade from both regions. It protected the Western empire from invasion from the Persians and the Ottomans, and practiced a more centralized rule than in the West. The Byzantines were famous for lavish art and architecture, as well as the Code of Justinian, which collected Roman law into a clear system.

Nicene Creed

The Byzantine Empire was Christian-based but incorporated Greek language, philosophy and literature and drew its law and government policies from Rome. However, there was as yet no unified doctrine of Christianity, as it was a relatively new religion that had spread rapidly and without a great deal of organization. In 325, the First Council of Nicaea addressed this issue. From this conference came the Nicene Creed, addressing the Trinity and other basic Christian beliefs. The Council of Chalcedon in 451 stated that any rejection of the Trinity was blasphemy.

Fall of the Western Roman Empire

Germanic tribes, including the Visigoths, Ostrogoths, Vandals, Saxons and Franks, controlled most of Europe. The Roman Empire faced major opposition on that front. The increasing size of the empire also made it harder to manage, leading to dissatisfaction throughout the empire as Roman government became less efficient. Germanic tribes refused to adhere to the Nicene Creed, instead following Arianism, which led the Roman Catholic Church to declare them heretics. The Franks proved a powerful military force in their defeat of the Muslims in 732. In 768, Charlemagne became king of the Franks. These tribes waged several wars against Rome, including the invasion of Britannia by the Angles and Saxons. Far-flung Rome lost control over this area of its Empire, and eventually Rome itself was invaded. Iconoclasm

Emperor Leo III ordered the destruction of all icons throughout the Byzantine Empire. Images of Jesus were replaced with a cross, and images of Jesus, Mary or other religious figures were considered blasphemy on grounds of idolatry. The current Pope, Gregory II, called a synod to discuss the issue. The synod declared that destroying these images was heretical, and that strong disciplinary measures would result for anyone who took this step. Leo's response was an attempt to kidnap Pope Gregory, but this plan ended in failure when his ships were destroyed by a storm.

Viking Invasions

Vikings invaded Northern France in the tenth century, eventually becoming the Normans. Originating in Scandinavia, the Vikings were accomplished seafarers with advanced knowledge of trade routes. With overpopulation plaguing their native lands, they began to travel. From the eighth to the eleventh centuries, they spread throughout Europe, conquering and colonizing. Vikings invaded and colonized England through several waves, including the Anglo-Saxon invasions that displaced Roman control. Their influence remained significant in England, affecting everything from the language of the country to place names and even the government and social structure. By 900, Vikings had settled in Iceland. They proceeded then to Greenland and eventually to North America, arriving in the New World even before the Spanish and British who claimed the lands several centuries later. They also traded with the Byzantine Empire until the eleventh century when their significant level of activity came to an end.

Tenth Century Events

In Europe, the tenth century is largely known as the Dark Ages, as numerous Viking invasions disrupted societies that had been more settled under Roman rule. Vikings settled in Northern France, eventually becoming the Normans. By the eleventh century, Europe would rise again into the High Middle Ages with the beginning of the Crusades.
In China, wars also raged. This led the Chinese to make use of gunpowder for the first time in warfare.

In the Americas, the Mayan Empire was winding down while the Toltec became more prominent. Pueblo Indian culture was also at its zenith.

In the East, the Muslims and the Byzantine Empire were experiencing a significant period of growth and development.

European Feudalism

A major element of the social and economic life of Europe, feudalism developed as a way to ensure European rulers would have the wherewithal to quickly raise an army when necessary. Vassals swore loyalty and promised to provide military service for lords, who in return offered a fief, or a parcel of land, for them to use to generate their livelihood. Vassals could work the land themselves, have it worked by peasants or serfs—workers who had few rights and were little more than slaves—or grant the fief to someone else. The king legally owned all the land, but in return promised to protect the vassals from invasion and war. Vassals returned a certain percentage of their income to the lords, who in turn passed a portion of their income on to the king. A similar practice was manorialism, in which the feudal system was applied to a self-contained manor. These manors were often owned by the lords who ran them, but were usually included in the same system of loyalty and promises of military service that drove feudalism.

Roman Catholic Church Influence

The Roman Catholic Church extended significant influence both politically and economically throughout medieval society. The church supplied education, as there were no established schools or universities. To a large extent, the church had filled a power void left by various invasions throughout the former Roman Empire, leading it to exercise a role that was far more political than religious. Kings were heavily influenced by the Pope and other church officials, and churches controlled large amounts of land throughout Europe.

Black Death

The Black Death, believed to be bubonic plague, came to Europe probably brought by fleas carried on rats that were regular passengers on sailing vessels. It killed in excess of a third of the entire population of Europe and effectively ended feudalism as a political system. Many who had formerly served as peasants or serfs found different work, as a demand for skilled labor grew. Nation-states grew in power, and in the face of the pandemic, many began to turn away from faith in God and toward the ideals of ancient Greece and Rome for government and other beliefs.

Crusades

The Crusades began in the eleventh century and progressed well into the twelfth. The major goal of these various military ventures was to slow the progression of Muslim forces into Europe and to expel them from the Holy Land, where they had taken control of Jerusalem and Palestine. Alexius I, the Eastern emperor, called for helped from Pope Urban II when Palestine was taken. In 1095, the Pope, hoping to reunite Eastern and Western Christian influences, encouraged all Christians to help the cause. Amidst great bloodshed, this Crusade recaptured Jerusalem, but over the next centuries, Jerusalem and other areas of the Holy Land changed hands numerous times. The Second Crusade, in 1145, consisted of an unsuccessful attempt to retake Damascus. The Third Crusade, under Pope Gregory VIII, attempted to recapture Jerusalem, but failed. The Fourth Crusade, under Pope Innocent III, attempted to come into the Holy Land via Egypt. The Crusades led to greater power for the Pope and the Catholic Church in general and also opened numerous trading and cultural routes between Europe and the East.

11th Century Developments

Politics in India

After the Mauryan dynasty, the Guptas ruled India, maintaining a long period of peace and prosperity in the area. During this time, the Indian people invented the decimal system as well as the concept of zero. They produced cotton and calico, as well as other products in high demand in Europe and Asia, and developed a complex system of medicine.

The Gupta Dynasty ended in the eleventh century with a Muslim invasion of the region. These sultans ruled for several centuries. Tamerlane, one of the most famous, expanded India's borders and founded the Mogul Dynasty. His grandson Akbar promoted freedom of religion and built a wide-spread number of mosques, forts, and other buildings throughout the country.

Chinese and Japanese governments

After the Mongols, led by Genghis Khan and his grandson Kublai Khan, unified the Mongol Empire, China was led by the Ming and Manchu Dynasties. Both these Dynasties were isolationist, ending China's interaction with other countries until the eighteenth century. The Ming Dynasty was known for its porcelain, while the Manchus focused on farming and road construction as the population grew.

Japan developed independent of China, but borrowed the Buddhist religion, the Chinese writing system, and other elements of Chinese society. Ruled by the divine emperor, Japan basically functioned on a feudal system led by Daimyos, or lords, and soldiers known as samurai. Japan remained isolationist, not interacting significantly with the rest of the world until the 1800s.

Africa

Only a few areas of Africa were amenable to habitation, due to the large amount of desert and other inhospitable terrain. Egypt remained important, though most of the northern coast became Muslim as their armies spread through the area. Ghana rose as a trade center in the ninth century, lasting into the twelfth century, primarily trading in gold, which it exchange for Saharan salt. Mali rose somewhat later, with the trade center Timbuktu becoming an important exporter of goods such as iron, leather and tin. Mali also dealt in agricultural trade, becoming one of the most significant trading centers in West Africa. The Muslim religion dominated, and technological advancement was sparse.

African culture was largely defined through migration, as Arab merchants and others settled on the continent, particularly along the east coast. Scholars from the Muslim nations gravitated to Timbuktu, which in addition to its importance in trade, had also become a magnet for those seeking knowledge and education.

Islam

Born in 570 CE, Mohammed became prominent in 610, leading his followers in a new religion called Islam, which means submission to God's will. Before this time, the Arabian Peninsula was inhabited largely by Bedouins, nomads who battled amongst each other and lived in tribal organizations. But by the time Mohammed died in 632, most of Arabia had become Muslim to some extent.

Mohammed conquered Mecca, where a temple called the Kaaba had long served as a center of the nomadic religions. He declared this temple the most sacred of Islam, and Mecca as the holy city. His writings became the Koran, or Qur'an, divine revelations he said had been delivered to him by the angel Gabriel.

Mohammed's teachings gave the formerly tribal Arabian people a sense of unity that had not existed in the area before. After his death, the converted Muslims of Arabia conquered a vast territory, creating an empire and bringing advances in literature, technology, science and art just as Europe was declining under the scourge of the Black Death. Literature from this period includes the *Arabian Nights* and the *Rubaiyat* of Omar Khayyam.
Later in its development, Islam split into two factions, the Shiite and the Sunni Muslims. Conflict continues today between these groups.

Ottoman Empire

By 1400, the Ottomans had grown in power in Anatolia and had begun attempts to take Constantinople. In 1453 they finally conquered the Byzantine capital and renamed it Istanbul. The Ottoman Empire's major strength, much like Rome before it, lay in its ability to unite widely disparate people through religious tolerance. This tolerance, which stemmed from the idea that Muslims, Christians, and Jews were fundamentally related and could coexist, enabled the Ottomans to develop a widely varied culture. They also believed in just laws and just government, with government centered in a monarch, known as the sultan.

World History from 1450 A.D. to the Present

Renaissance

Renaissance literally means "rebirth." After the darkness of the Dark Ages and the Black Plague, interest rose again in the beliefs and politics of ancient Greece and Rome. Art, literature, music, science, and philosophy all burgeoned during the Renaissance.

Many of the ideas of the Renaissance began in Florence, Italy, spurred by the Medici family. Education for the upper classes expanded to include law, math, reading, writing, and classical Greek and Roman works. As the Renaissance progressed, the world was presented through art and literature in a realistic way that had never been explored before. This realism drove culture to new heights.

Artists, authors and scientists

Artists of the Renaissance included Leonardo da Vinci, also an inventor, Michelangelo, also an architect, and others who focused on realism in their work. In literature, major contributions came from the humanist, authors like Petrarch, Erasmus, Sir Thomas More, and Boccaccio, who believed man should focus on reality rather than on the ethereal. Shakespeare, Cervantes and Dante followed in their footsteps, and their works found a wide audience thanks to Gutenberg's development of the printing press.

Scientific developments of the Renaissance included the work of Copernicus, Galileo and Kepler, who challenged the geocentric philosophies of the church by proving the earth was not the center of the solar system.

Reformation

The Reformation consisted of the Protestant Revolution and the Catholic Reformation. The Protestant Revolution rose in Germany when Martin Luther protested abuses of the Catholic Church. John Calvin led the movement in Switzerland, while in England King Henry VIII made use of the Revolution's ideas to further his own political goals. The Catholic Reformation occurred in response to the Protestant Revolution, leading to various changes in the Catholic Church. Some provided wider tolerance of different religious viewpoints, but others actually increased the persecution of those deemed to be heretics.

From a religious standpoint, the Reformation occurred due to abuses by the Catholic Church such as indulgences and dispensations, religious offices being offered up for sale, and an increasingly dissolute clergy. Politically, the Reformation was driven by increased power of various ruling monarchs, who wished to take all power to themselves rather than allowing power to remain with the church. They also had begun to chafe at papal taxes and the church's increasing wealth. The ideas of the Protestant Revolution removed power from the Catholic Church and the Pope himself, playing nicely into the hands of those monarchs, such as Henry VIII, who wanted out from under the church's control.

Scientific Revolution

In addition to holding power in the political realm, church doctrine also governed scientific belief. During the Scientific Revolution, astronomers and other scientists began to amass evidence that challenged the church's scientific doctrines. Major figures of the Scientific Revolution included:

Nicolaus Copernicus—wrote *Revolutions of the Celestial Spheres*, arguing that the Earth revolved around the sun.

Tycho Brahe—catalogued astronomical observations.

Johannes Kepler—developed Laws of Planetary Motions.

Galileo Galilei—defended the heliocentric theories of Copernicus and Kepler, discovered four moons of Jupiter, and died under house arrest by the Church, charged with heresy.

Isaac Newton—discovered gravity, studied optics, calculus and physics, and believed the workings of nature could be observed, studied, and proven through observation.

Enlightenment

During the Enlightenment, philosophers and scientists began to rely more and more on observation to support their ideas, rather than building on past beliefs, particularly those held by the church. A focus on ethics and logic drove their work. Major philosophers of the Enlightenment included:

Rene Descartes—"I think, therefore I am." He believed strongly in logic and rules of observation.

David Hume—pioneered empiricism and skepticism, believing that truth could only be found through direct experience, and that what others said to be true was always suspect.

Immanuel Kant—believed in self-examination and observation, and that the root of morality lay within human beings.

Jean-Jacques Rousseau—developed the idea of the social contract, that government existed by the agreement of the people, and that the government was obligated to protect the people and their basic rights. His ideas influenced John Locke and Thomas Jefferson.

American and French Revolutions

Both the American and French Revolution came about as a protest against the excesses and overly controlling nature of their respective monarchs. In America, the British colonies had been left mostly self-governing until the British monarchs began to increase control, leading the colonies to revolt. In France, the nobility's excesses had led to increasingly difficult economic conditions, with inflation, heavy taxation and food shortages creating horrible burdens on the people. Both revolutions led to the development of republics to replace the monarchies that were displaced. However, the French Revolution eventually led to the rise of the dictator Napoleon Bonaparte, while the American Revolution produced a working republic from the beginning.

In 1789, King Louis XVI, faced with a huge national debt, convened parliament. The Third Estate, or Commons, a division of the French parliament, then claimed power, and the king's resistance led to the storming of the Bastille, the royal prison. The people established a constitutional monarchy. When King Louis XVI and Marie Antoinette attempted to leave the country, they were executed on the guillotine. From 1793 to 1794, Robespierre and extreme radicals, the Jacobins, instituted a Reign of Terror, executing thousands of nobles as well as anyone considered an enemy of the Revolution. Robespierre was then executed, as well, and the Directory came into power. This governing body proved incompetent and

- 26 -

corrupt, allowing Napoleon Bonaparte to come to power in 1799, first as a dictator, then as emperor. While the French Revolution threw off the power of a corrupt monarchy, its immediate results were likely not what the original perpetrators of the revolt had intended.

1905 Russian Revolution

In Russia, rule lay in the hands of the Czars, and the overall structure was feudalistic. Beneath the Czars was a group of rich nobles, landowners whose lands were worked by peasants and serfs. The Russo-Japanese War (1904-1905) made conditions much worse for the lower classes. When peasants demonstrated outside the Czar's Winter Palace, the palace guard fired upon the crowd. The demonstration had been organized by a trade union leader, and after the violent response, many unions as well as political parties blossomed and began to lead numerous strikes. When the economy ground to a halt, Czar Nicholas II signed a document known as the October Manifesto, which established a constitutional monarchy and gave legislative power to parliament. However, he violated the Manifesto shortly thereafter, disbanding parliament and ignoring the civil liberties granted by the Manifesto. This eventually led to the Bolshevik Revolution of 1917.

1917 Bolshevik Revolution

Throughout its modern history, Russia had lagged behind other countries in development. The continued existence of a feudal system, combined with harsh conditions and the overall size of the country, led to massive food shortages and increasingly harsh conditions for the majority of the population. The tyrannical rule favored by the Czars only made this worse, as did repeated losses in various military conflicts. Increasing poverty, decreasing supplies, and the Czar's violation of the October Manifesto which had given some political power and civil rights to the people finally came to a head with the Bolshevik Revolution.

Major events
A workers' strike in Petrograd in 1917 set the revolutionary wheels in motion when the army sided with the workers. While parliament set up a provisional government made up of nobles, the workers and military joined to form their own governmental system known as soviets, which consisted of local councils elected by the people. The ensuing chaos opened the doors for formerly exiled leaders Vladimir Lenin, Joseph Stalin and Leon Trotsky to move in and gain popular support as well as the support of the Red Guard. Overthrowing parliament, they took power, creating a communist state in Russia. This development led to the spread of Communism throughout Eastern Europe and elsewhere, greatly affecting diplomatic policies throughout the world for several decades.

Industrial Revolution

The Industrial Revolution began in Great Britain, bringing coal- and steam-powered machinery into widespread use. Industry began a period of rapid growth with these developments. Goods that had previously been produced in small workshops or even in homes were produced more efficiently and in much larger quantities in factories. Where society had been largely agrarian based, the focus swiftly shifted to an industrial outlook. As electricity and internal combustion engines replaced coal and steam as energy sources, even more drastic and rapid changes occurred. Western European countries in particular turned to colonialism, taking control of portions of Africa and Asia to assure access to the raw materials needed to produce factory goods. Specialized labor became very much in demand, and businesses grew rapidly, creating monopolies, increasing world trade, and creating large urban centers. Even agriculture changed fundamentally as the Industrial Revolution led to a second Agricultural Revolution as the addition of the new technologies advanced agricultural production.

<u>First and second phases</u>
The first phase of the Industrial Revolution took place from roughly 1750 to 1830. The textile industry experienced major changes as more and more elements of the process became mechanized. Mining benefited from the steam engine. Transportation became easier and more widely available as waterways were improved and the railroad came into prominence. In the second phase, from 1830 to 1910, industries further improved in efficiency and new industries were introduced as photography, various chemical processes, and electricity became more widely available to produce new goods or new, improved versions of old goods. Petroleum and hydroelectric became major sources of power. During this time, the industrial revolution spread out of Western Europe and into the US and Japan.

<u>Political, social and economic side effects</u>
The Industrial Revolution led to widespread education, a wider franchise, and the development of mass communication in the political arena. Economically, conflicts arose between companies and their employees, as struggles for fair treatment and fair wages increased. Unions gained power and became more active. Government regulation over industries increased, but at the same time, growing businesses fought for the right to free enterprise. In the social sphere, populations increased and began to concentrate around centers of industry. Cities became larger and more densely populated. Scientific advancements led to more efficient agriculture, greater supply of goods, and increased knowledge of medicine and sanitation, leading to better overall health.

18th and 19th Century Nationalism

Nationalism, put simply, is a strong belief in, identification with, and allegiance to a particular nation and people. Nationalistic belief unified various areas that had previously seen themselves as fragmented which led to patriotism and, in some cases, imperialism. As nationalism grew, individual nations sought to grow, bringing in other, smaller states that shared similar characteristics such as language and cultural beliefs. Unfortunately, a major side effect of these growing nationalistic beliefs was often conflict and outright war.

In Europe, imperialism led countries to spread their influence into Africa and Asia. Africa was eventually divided among several European countries that needed the raw materials to be found there. Asia also came under European control, with the exception of China, Japan and Siam (now Thailand). In the US, Manifest Destiny became the rallying cry as the country expanded west. Italy and Germany formed larger nations from a variety of smaller states.
WWI

<u>Europe</u>
WW I began in 1914 with the assassination of Archduke Franz Ferdinand, heir to the throne of Austria-Hungary, by a Serbian national. This led to a conflict between Austria-Hungary and Serbia that quickly escalated into the First World War. Europe split into the Allies— Britain, France and Russia, and later Italy, Japan and the US, against the Central Powers— Austria-Hungary, Germany and Turkey. As the war spread, countries beyond Europe became involved. The war left Europe deeply in debt, and particularly devastated the

- 28 -

German economy. The ensuing Great Depression made matters worse, and economic devastation opened the door for Communist, Fascist and Socialist governments to gain power.

Trench warfare
Fighting during WW I took place largely in a series of trenches built along the Eastern and Western Fronts. These trenches added up to about 24,000 miles, each side having dug at least 12,000 miles' worth during the course of the war. This produced fronts that stretched nearly 400 miles, from the coast of Belgium to the border of Switzerland. The Allies made use of straightforward open-air trenches with a front line, supporting lines, and communications lines. By contrast, the German trenches sometimes included well-equipped underground living quarters.

Communism and Socialism

At their roots, socialism and communism both focus on public ownership and distribution of goods and services. However, communism works toward revolution by drawing on what it sees to be inevitable class antagonism, eventually overthrowing the upper classes and the systems of capitalism. Socialism makes use of democratic procedures, building on the existing order. This was particularly true of the Utopian-Socialists, who saw industrial capitalism as oppressive, not allowing workers to prosper. While socialism struggled between the World Wars, communism took hold, especially in Eastern Europe. After WW II, democratic socialism became more common. Later, capitalism took a stronger hold again, and today most industrialized countries in the world function under an economy that mixes elements of capitalism and socialism.

Nazi Party Rise

The Great Depression had a particularly devastating effect on Germany's economy, especially after the US was no longer able to supply reconstruction loans to help the country regain its footing. With unemployment rising rapidly, dissatisfaction with the government grew. Fascist and Communist parties rose, promising change and improvement. Led by Adolf Hitler, the Fascist, Nazi Party eventually gained power in Parliament based on these promises and the votes of desperate German workers. When Hitler became Chancellor, he launched numerous expansionist policies, violating the peace treaties that had ended WW I. His military buildup and conquering of neighboring countries sparked the aggression that soon led to WW II.

Blitzkrieg

The blitzkrieg, or "lightning war," consisted of fast, powerful surprise attacks that disrupted communications, made it difficult if not impossible for the victims to retaliate, and demoralized Germany's foes. The "blitz," or the aerial bombing of England in 1940, was one example, with bombings occurring in London and other cities 57 nights in a row. The Battle of Britain, from 1940 to 1941, also brought intense raids by Germany's air force, the Luftwaffe, mostly targeting ports and British air force bases. Eventually, Britain's Royal Air Force blocked the Luftwaffe, ending Germany's hopes for conquering Britain.

Battle of the Bulge

Following the D-Day Invasion, Allied forces gained considerable ground, and began a major campaign to push through Europe. In December of 1944, Hitler launched a counteroffensive, attempting to retake Antwerp, an important port. The ensuing battle became the largest land battle on the war's Western Front, and was known as the Battle of the Ardennes, or the Battle of the Bulge. The battle lasted from December 16, 1944 to January 28, 1945. The Germans pushed forward, making inroads into Allied lines, but in the end the Allies brought the advance to a halt. The Germans were pushed back, with massive losses on both sides. However, those losses proved crippling to the German army.

Holocaust

As Germany sank deeper and deeper into dire economic straits, the tendency was to look for a person or group of people to blame for the problems of the country. With distrust of the Jewish people already ingrained, it was easy for German authorities to set up the Jews as scapegoats for Germany's problems. Under the rule of Hitler and the Nazi party, the "Final Solution" for the supposed Jewish problem was devised. Millions of Jews, as well as Gypsies, homosexuals, Communists, Catholics, the mentally ill and others, simply named as criminals, were transported to concentration camps during the course of the war. At least six million were slaughtered in death camps such as Auschwitz, where horrible conditions and torture of prisoners were commonplace. The Allies were aware of rumors of mass slaughter throughout the war, but many discounted the reports. Only when troops went in to liberate the prisoners was the true horror of the concentration camps brought to light.

The Holocaust resulted in massive loss of human life, but also in the loss and destruction of cultures. Because the genocide focused on specific ethnic groups, many traditions, histories, knowledge, and other cultural elements were lost, particularly among the Jewish and Gypsy populations. After World War II, the United Nations recognized genocide as a "crime against humanity." The UN passed the Universal Declaration of Human Rights in order to further specify what rights the organization protected. Nazi war criminals faced justice during the Nuremberg Trials. There individuals, rather than their governments, were held accountable for war crimes.

Cold War

With millions of military and civilian deaths and over 12 million persons displaced, WW II left large regions of Europe and Asia in disarray. Communist governments moved in with promises of renewed prosperity and economic stability. The Soviet Union backed Communist regimes in much of Eastern Europe. In China, Mao Zedong led communist forces in the overthrow of the Chinese Nationalist Party and instituted a Communist government in 1949. While the new Communist governments restored a measure of stability to much of Eastern Europe, it brought its own problems, with dictatorial governments and an oppressive police force. The spread of Communism also led to several years of tension between Communist countries and the democratic west, as the west fought to slow the spread of oppressive regimes throughout the world. With both sides in possession of nuclear weapons, tensions rose. Each side feared the other would resort to nuclear attack. This standoff lasted until 1989, when the Berlin Wall fell. The Soviet Union was dissolved two years later.

United Nations

The United Nations (UN) came into being toward the end of World War II. A successor to the less-than-successful League of Nations, formed after World War I, the UN built and improved on those ideas. Since its inception, the UN has worked to bring the countries of the world together for diplomatic solutions to international problems, including sanctions and other restrictions. It has also initiated military action, calling for peacekeeping troops from member countries to move against countries violating UN policies.

One example of UN involvement in an international conflict is the Korean War, the first war in which an international alliance of this kind was actively involved.

Decolonization

A rise of nationalism among European colonies led to many of them declaring independence. India and Pakistan became independent of Britain at this time, and numerous African and Asian colonies declared independence, as well. This period of decolonization lasted into the 1960s. Some colonies moved successfully into independence but many, especially in Africa and Asia, struggled to create stable governments and economies, and suffered from ethnic and religious conflicts. Some of those countries still struggle today.

Korean War

In 1910, Japan annexed Korea and maintained this control until 1945, when Soviet and US troops occupied the country. The Soviet Union controlled North Korea, while the US controlled South Korea. In 1947, the UN ordered elections in Korea to unify the country but the Soviet Union refused to allow them to take place, instead setting up a communist government in North Korea. In 1950, the US withdrew troops, and the North Korean troops moved to invade South Korea. The Korean War was the first war in which the UN—or any international organization—played a major role. The US, Australia, Canada, France, Netherlands, Great Britain, Turkey, China, USSR and other countries sent troops at various times, for both sides, throughout the war. In 1953, the war ended in a truce, but no peace agreement was ever achieved, and Korea remains divided.

Vietnam War

Vietnam had previously been part of a French colony called French Indochina. The Vietnam War began with the French Indochina War from 1946-1954, in which France battled with the Democratic Republic of Vietnam, ruled by Ho Chi Minh.

In 1954, a siege at Dien Bien Phu ended in a Vietnamese victory. Vietnam was then divided into North and South, much like Korea. Communist forces controlled the North and the South was controlled by South Vietnamese forces, supported by the US. Conflict ensued, leading to a war. US troops eventually lead the fight, in support of South Vietnam. The war became a major political issue in the US, with many citizens protesting American involvement. In 1976, South Vietnam surrendered, and Vietnam became the Socialist Republic of Vietnam.

Globalism

In the modern era, globalism has emerged as a popular political ideology. Globalism is based in the idea that all people and all nations are interdependent. Each nation is dependent on one or more other nations for production of and markets for goods, and for income generation. Today's ease of international travel and communication, including technological advances such as the airplane, has heightened this sense of interdependence. The global economy, and the general idea of globalism, has shaped many economic and political choices since the beginning of the twentieth century. Many of today's issues, including environmental awareness, economic struggles, and continued warfare, often require the cooperation of many countries if they are to be dealt with effectively.

Globalization Effects

With countries worldwide often seeking the same resources, some, particularly nonrenewable resources, have experienced high demand. At times this has resulted in wild price fluctuations. One major example is the demand for petroleum products such as oil and natural gas. Increased travel and communication make it possible to deal with diseases in remote locations; however, it also allows diseases to be spread via travelers, as well.

A major factor contributing to increased globalization over the past few decades has been the Internet. By allowing instantaneous communication with anyone nearly anywhere on the globe, the Internet has led to interaction between far-flung individuals and countries, and an ever increasing awareness of happenings all over the world.

Middle East Relations and Economics

Its location on the globe, with ease of access to Europe and Asia, and its preponderance of oil deposits, makes the middle eastern countries a crucial factor in many international issues both diplomatic and economic. Because of its central location, the Middle East has been a hotbed for violence since before the beginning of recorded history. Conflicts over land, resources, religious and political power continue in the area today, spurred by conflict over control of the area's vast oil fields as well as over territories that have been disputed for literally hundreds—and even thousands—of years.

Genocide

The three major occurrences of genocide in modern history other than the Holocaust are as follows:
Armenian genocide—occurred in the 1900s when the Young Turks, heirs to the Ottoman Empire, slaughtered over a million Armenians between 1915 and 1917. This constituted nearly half the Armenian population at the time.
Russian purges under Stalin—Scholars have attributed deaths between 3 and 60 million, both directly and indirectly, to the policies and edicts of Joseph Stalin's regime. The deaths took place from 1921 to 1953, when Stalin died. In recent years, many scholars have settled on a number of deaths near 20 million but this is still disputed today.
Rwandan Genocide—in 1994, hundreds of thousands of Tutsi and Hutu sympathizers were slaughtered during the Rwandan Civil War. The UN did not act or authorize intervention during these atrocities.

United States History to 1877

Well-Known Native Americans

The following are five well-known Native Americans and their roles in early U.S. history:
- Squanto, an Algonquian, helped early English settlers survive the hard winter by teaching them the native methods of planting corn, squash, and pumpkins.
- Pocahontas, also Algonquian, became famous as a liaison with John Smith's Jamestown colony in 1607.
- Sacagawea, a Shoshone, served a vital role in the Lewis and Clark expedition when the two explorers hired her as their guide in 1805.
- Crazy Horse and Sitting Bull led Sioux and Cheyenne troops in the Battle of the Little Bighorn in 1876, soundly defeating George Armstrong Custer.
- Chief Joseph, a leader of the Nez Perce who supported peaceful interaction with white settlers, attempted to relocate his tribe to Canada rather than move them to a reservation.

Native American Groups

The major regional Native American groups and the major traits of each one are as follows:
- The Algonquians in the eastern part of the United States lived in wigwams. The northern tribes subsisted on hunting and gathering, while those who were farther south grew crops such as corn.
- The Iroquois, also an east coast tribe, spoke a different language from the Algonquians, and lived in rectangular longhouses.
- The Plains tribes lived between the Mississippi River and the Rocky Mountains. Nomadic tribes, they lived in teepees and followed the buffalo herds. Plains tribes included the Sioux, Cheyenne, Comanche and Blackfoot.
- Pueblo tribes included the Zuni, Hope, and Acoma. They lived in the Southwest deserts in homes made of stone or adobe. They domesticated animals and cultivated corn and beans.
- On the Pacific coast, tribes such as the Tlingit, Chinook and Salish lived on fish as well as deer, native berries and roots. Their rectangular homes housed large family groups, and they used totem poles.
- In the far north, the Aleuts and Inuit lived in skin tents or igloos. Talented fishermen, they built kayaks and umiaks and also hunted caribou, seals, whales and walrus.

Age of Exploration

The Age of Exploration is also called the Age of Discovery. It is generally considered to have begun in the early fifteenth century, and continued into the seventeenth century. Major developments of the Age of Exploration included technological advances in navigation, mapmaking and shipbuilding. These advances led to expanded European exploration of the rest of the world. Explorers set out from several European countries, including Portuguese, Spain, France and England, seeking new routes to Asia. These efforts led to the discovery of new lands, as well as colonization in India, Asia, Africa, and North America.

Navigational Tools

For long ocean journeys, it was important for sailors to be able to find their way home even when their vessels sailed far out to sea, well out of sight of land. A variety of navigational tools enabled them to launch ambitious journeys over long distances. The compass and astrolabe were particularly important advancements. The magnetic compass had been used by Chinese navigators for some time, and knowledge of the astrolabe came to Europe from Arab navigators and traders who had refined designs developed by the ancient Greeks. The Portuguese developed a ship called a caravel in the 1400s that incorporated navigational advancements with the ability to make long sea journeys. Equipped with this advanced vessel, the Portuguese achieved a major goal of the Age of Exploration by discovering a sea route from Europe to Asia in 1498.

Christopher Columbus

In 1492, Columbus, a Genoan explorer, obtained financial backing from King Ferdinand and Queen Isabella of Spain to seek a sea route to Asia. He sought a trade route with the Asian Indies to the west. With three ships, the *Niña*, the *Pinta* and the *Santa Maria*, he eventually landed in the West Indies. While Columbus failed in his effort to discover a western route to Asia, he is credited with the discovery of the Americas.

Colonization of the Americas

The following are the various goals of the French, Spanish, Dutch and British in the colonization of the Americas:
- Initial French colonies were focused on expanding the fur trade. Later, French colonization led to the growth of plantations in Louisiana which brought numerous African slaves to the New World.
- Spanish colonists came to look for wealth, and to converting the natives to Christianity. For some, the desire for gold led to mining in the New World, while others established large ranches.
- The Dutch were also involved in the fur trade, and also imported slaves as the need for laborers increased.
- British colonists arrived with various goals. Some were simply looking for additional income, while others were fleeing Britain to escape religious persecution.

New England colonies
The New England colonies were: New Hampshire, Connecticut, Rhode Island and Massachusetts. The colonies in New England were founded largely to escape religious persecution in England. The beliefs of the Puritans, who migrated to America in the 1600s, significantly influenced the development of these colonies. Situated in the northeast coastal areas of America, the New England colonies featured numerous harbors as well as dense forest. The soil, however, is rocky and, with a very short growing season, was not well suited for agriculture. The economy of New England during the colonial period centered around fishing, shipbuilding and trade along with some small farms and lumber mills. Although some groups congregated in small farms, life centered largely on towns and cities where merchants largely controlled the trade economy. Coastal cities such as Boston grew and thrived.

Middle or Middle Atlantic Colonies

The Middle or Middle Atlantic Colonies were: New York, New Jersey, Pennsylvania and Delaware. Unlike the New England colonies, where most colonists were from England and Scotland, the Middle Colonies founders were from various countries including the Netherlands, Holland and Sweden. Various factors led these colonists to America. More fertile than New England, the Middle Colonies became major producers of crops included rye, oats, potatoes, wheat, and barley. Some particularly wealthy inhabitants owned large farms and/or businesses. Farmers in general were able to produce enough to have a surplus to sell. Tenant farmers also rented land from larger land owners.

Southern Colonies

The Southern Colonies were Maryland, Virginia, North Carolina, South Carolina and Georgia. Of the Southern Colonies, Virginia was the first permanent English colony and Georgia the last. The warm climate and rich soil of the south encouraged agriculture, and the growing season was long. As a result, economy in the south was based largely on labor-intensive plantations. Crops included tobacco, rice and indigo, all of which became valuable cash crops. Most land in the south was controlled by wealthy plantation owners and farmers. Labor on the farms came in the form of indentured servants and African slaves. The first of these African slaves arrived in Virginia in 1619, starting a long, unpleasant history of slavery in the American colonies.

French and Indian Wars

The British defeat of the Spanish Armada in 1588 led to the decline of Spanish power in Europe. This in turn led the British and French into battle over several wars between 1689 and 1748. These wars were:

- King William's War, or the Nine Years War, 1689-1697. This war was fought largely in Flanders.
- The War of Spanish Succession, or Queen Anne's War, 1702-1713
- War of Austrian Succession, or King George's War, 1740-1748

The fourth and final, the French and Indian War, was fought largely in the North American territory, and resulted in the end of France's reign as a colonial power in North America. Although the French held many advantages, including more cooperative colonists and numerous Indian allies, the strong leadership of William Pitt eventually led the British to victory. Costs incurred during the wars eventually led to discontent in the colonies. This helped spark the American Revolution

Navigation Acts

Enacted in 1651, the Navigation Acts were an attempt by Britain to dominate international trade. Aimed largely at the Dutch, the Acts banned foreign ships from transporting goods to the British colonies, and from transporting goods to Britain from elsewhere in Europe. While the restrictions on trade angered some colonists, these Acts were helpful to other American colonists who, as members of the British Empire, were legally able to provide ships for Britain's growing trade interests and use the ships for their own trading ventures. By the time the French and Indian War had ended, one-third of British merchant ships were built in the American colonies. Many colonists amassed fortunes in the shipbuilding trade.

Higher Taxes

The French and Indian War created circumstances for which the British desperately needed more revenue. These included:
- The need to pay off the war debt.
- The need for funds to defend the expanding empire
- The need for funds to govern Britain's thirty-three far-flung colonies, including the American colonies

These needs led the British to pass additional laws to increase revenues from the colonies. Because they had spent so much money to defend the American colonies, the British felt it was appropriate to collect considerably higher taxes from them. The colonists felt this was unfair, and many were led to protest the increasing taxes. Eventually, protest led to violence.

Triangular Trade

Triangular trade began in the Colonies with ships setting off for Africa carrying rum. In Africa, the rum was traded for gold or slaves. Ships then went from Africa to the West Indies, trading slaves for sugar, molasses, or money. To complete the triangle, the ships returned to the colonies with sugar or molasses to make more rum, as well as stores of gold and silver. This trade triangle violated the Molasses Act of 1733, which required the colonists to pay high duties to Britain on molasses acquired from French, Dutch, and Spanish colonies. The colonists ignored these duties, and the British government adopted a policy of salutary neglect by not enforcing them.

British-Colonial Relations

While earlier revenue-generating acts such as the Navigation Acts brought money to the colonists, the new laws after 1763 required colonists to pay money back to Britain. The British felt this was fair since the colonists were British subjects and since they had incurred debt protecting the Colonies. The colonists felt it was not only unfair, but illegal.

The development of local government in America had given the colonists a different view of the structure and role of government. This made it difficult for the British to understand colonist's protests against what the British felt was a fair and reasonable solution to the mother country's financial problems.

Colonist Discontent

More and more colonists had been born on American soil, decreasing any sense of kinship with the far away British rulers. Their new environment had led to new ideas of government and a strong view of the colonies as a separate entity from Britain. Colonists were allowed to self-govern in domestic issues, but Britain controlled international issues. In fact, the American colonies were largely left to form their own local government bodies, giving them more freedom than any other colonial territory. This gave the colonists a sense of independence which led them to resent control from Britain. Threats during the French and Indian War led the colonists to call for unification in order to protect themselves.

Colonial Government vs. British Government

As new towns and other legislative districts developed in America, the colonists began to practice representative government. Colonial legislative bodies were made up of elected representatives chosen by male property owners in the districts. These individuals represented interests of the districts from which they had been elected.

By contrast, in Britain the Parliament represented the entire country. Parliament was not elected to represent individual districts. Instead, they represented specific classes. Because of this drastically different approach to government, the British did not understand the colonists' statement that they had no representation in the British Parliament.

British Parliament Acts

Four major Acts of British Parliament that occurred after the French and Indian Wars and what they governed are:
- The Quartering Act, 1765. This act required colonists to provide accommodations and supplies for British troops. In addition, colonists were prohibited from settling west of the Appalachians until given permission by Britain.
- The Sugar Act, 1764. This act not only required taxes to be collected on molasses brought into the colonies, but gave British officials the right to search the homes of anyone suspected of violating it.
- The Stamp Act, 1765. The Stamp Act taxed printed materials such as newspapers and legal documents. Protests led the Stamp Act to be repealed in 1766, but the repeal also included the Declaratory Act, which stated that Parliament had the right to govern the colonies.
- The Townshend Acts, 1767. These acts taxed paper, paint, lead and tea that came into the colonies. Colonists led boycotts in protest, and in Massachusetts leaders like Samuel and John Adams began to organize resistance against British rule.

Boston Massacre

With the passage of the Stamp Act, nine colonies met in New York to demand its repeal. Elsewhere, protest arose in New York City, Philadelphia, Boston and other cities. These protests sometimes escalated into violence, often targeting ruling British officials. The passage of the Townshend Acts in 1767 led to additional tension in the colonies. The British sent troops to New York City and Boston. On March 5, 1770, protesters began to taunt the British troops, throwing snowballs. The soldiers responded by firing into the crowd. This clash between protesters and soldiers led to five deaths and eight injuries, and was christened the Boston Massacre. Shortly thereafter, Britain repealed the majority of the Townshend Acts.

Tea Act and the Boston Tea Party

The majority of the Townshend Acts were repealed after the Boston Massacre in 1770, but Britain kept the tax on tea. In 1773, the Tea Act was passed. This allowed the East India Company to sell tea for much lower prices, and also allowed them to bypass American distributors, selling directly to shopkeepers instead. Colonial tea merchants saw this as a direct assault on their business. In December of 1773, 150 merchants boarded ships in

Boston Harbor and dumped 342 chests of tea into the sea in protest of the new laws. This act of protest came to be known as the Boston Tea Party.

Coercive Acts

The Coercive Acts passed by Britain in 1774 were meant to punish Massachusetts for defying British authority. The four Coercive Acts:
- Shut down ports in Boston until the city paid back the value of the tea destroyed during the Boston Tea Party.
- Required that local government officials in Massachusetts be appointed by the governor rather than being elected by the people.
- Allowed trials of British soldiers to be transferred to Britain rather than being held in Massachusetts.
- Required locals to provide lodging for British soldiers any time there was a disturbance, even if lodging required them to stay in private homes.

These Acts led to the assembly of the First Continental Congress in Philadelphia on September 5, 1774. Fifty-five delegates met, representing 12 of the American colonies. They sought compromise with England over England's increasingly harsh efforts to control the colonies.

First Continental Congress

The First Continental Congress met in Philadelphia on September 5, 1774. Their goal was to achieve a peaceful agreement with Britain. Made up of delegates from 12 of the 13 colonies, the Congress affirmed loyalty to Britain and the power of Parliament to dictate foreign affairs in the colonies. However, they demanded that the Intolerable Acts be repealed, and instituted a trade embargo with Britain until this came to pass.

In response, George III of Britain declared that the American colonies must submit or face military action. The British sought to end assemblies opposing their policies. These assemblies gathered weapons and began to form militias. On April 19, 1775, the British military was ordered to disperse a meeting of the Massachusetts Assembly. A battle ensued on Lexington Common as the armed colonists resisted. The resulting battles became the Battle of Lexington and Concord—the first battles of the American Revolution.

Second Continental Congress

The Second Continental Congress met in Philadelphia on May 10, 1775, a month after Lexington and Concord. Their discussions centered on defense of the American colonies and how to conduct the growing war, as well as local government. The delegates also discussed declaring independence from Britain, with many members in favor of this drastic move. They established an army, and on June 15, named George Washington as its commander in chief. By 1776, it was obvious that there was no turning back from full-scale war with Britain. The colonial delegates of the Continental Congress drafted the Declaration of Independence on July 4, 1776.

Revolutionary War Battles

The following are five battles of the Revolutionary War and their significance:

- The Battle of Lexington and Concord (April, 1775) is considered the first engagement of the Revolutionary War.
- The Battle of Bunker Hill, in June of 1775, was one of the bloodiest of the entire war. Although American troops withdrew, about half the British army was lost. The colonists proved they could stand against professional British soldiers. In August, Britain declared that the American colonies were officially in a state of rebellion.
- The first colonial victory occurred in Trenton, New Jersey, when Washington and his troops crossed the Delaware River on Christmas Day, 1776 for a December 26, surprise attack on British and Hessian troops.
- The Battle of Saratoga effectively ended a plan to separate the New England colonies from their Southern counterparts. The surrender of British general John Burgoyne led to France joining the war as allies of the Americans, and is generally considered a turning point of the war.
- On October 19, 1781, General Cornwallis surrendered after a defeat in the Battle of Yorktown, Virginia, ending the Revolutionary War.

Declaration of Independence

Penned by Thomas Jefferson and signed on July 4, 1776, the Declaration of Independence stated that King George III had violated the rights of the colonists and was establishing a tyrannical reign over them. Many of Jefferson's ideas of natural rights and property rights were shaped by seventeenth century philosopher John Locke. Jefferson focused on natural rights, as demonstrated by the assertion of people's rights to "life, liberty and the pursuit of happiness." Locke's comparable idea asserted "life, liberty, and private property." Both felt that the purpose of government was to protect the rights of the people, and that individual rights were more important than individuals' obligations to the state.

Treaty of Paris

The Treaty of Paris was signed on September 3, 1783, bringing an official end to the Revolutionary War. In this document, Britain officially recognized the United States of America as an independent nation. The treaty established the Mississippi River as the country's western border. The treaty also restored Florida to Spain, while France reclaimed African and Caribbean colonies seized by the British in 1763. On November 24, 1783, the last British troops departed from the newly born United States of America.

Articles of Confederation

A precursor to the Constitution, the Articles of Confederation represented the first attempt of the newly independent colonies to establish the basics of independent government. The Continental Congress passed the Articles on November 15, 1777. They went into effect on March 1, 1781, following ratification by the thirteen states.
The Articles prevented a central government from gaining too much power, instead giving power to a Congressional body made up of delegates from all thirteen states. However, the individual states retained final authority.

Without a strong central executive, though, this weak alliance among the new states proved ineffective in settling disputes or enforcing laws. The idea of a weak central government needed to be revised. Recognition of these weaknesses eventually led to the drafting of a new document, the Constitution.

Constitution

Delegates from twelve of the thirteen states (Rhode Island was not represented) met in Philadelphia in May of 1787, initially intending to revise the Articles of Confederation. However, it quickly became apparent that a simple revision would not provide the workable governmental structure the newly formed country needed. After vowing to keep all the proceedings secret until the final document was completed, the delegates set out to draft what would eventually become the Constitution of the United States of America. By keeping the negotiations secret, the delegates were able to present a completed document to the country for ratification, rather than having every small detail hammered out by the general public.

Proposed Government Structure

The delegates agreed that the new nation required a strong central government, but that its overall power should be limited. The various branches of the government should have balanced power, so that no one group could control the others. Final power belonged with the citizens who voted officials into office based on who would provide the best representation.

Virginia Plan, New Jersey Plan, and the Great Compromise

Disagreement immediately occurred between delegates from large states and those from smaller states. The governor of Virginia, Edmond Randolph, felt that representation in Congress should be based on state population. This was the Virginia Plan. The New Jersey Plan, presented by William Paterson, from New Jersey, proposed each state have equal representation. Finally, Roger Sherman from Connecticut formulated the Connecticut Compromise, also called the Great Compromise. The result was the familiar structure we have today. Each state has the equal representation of two Senators in the Senate, with the number of representatives in the House of Representatives based on population. This is called a bicameral Congress. Both houses may draft bills, but financial matters must originate in the House of Representatives.

Three-Fifths Compromise

During debate on the U.S. Constitution, a disagreement arose between the Northern and Southern states involving how slaves should be counted when determining a state's quota of representatives. In the South large numbers of slaves were commonly used to run plantations. Delegates wanted slaves to be counted to determine the number of representatives, but not counted to determine the amount of taxes the states would pay. The Northern states wanted exactly the opposite arrangement. The final decision was to count three-fifths of the slave population both for tax purposes and to determine representation. This was called the three-fifths compromise.

Commerce Compromise

The Commerce Compromise also resulted from a North/South disagreement. In the North the economy was centered on industry and trade. The Southern economy was largely agricultural. The Northern states wanted to give the new government the ability to regulate exports as well as trade between the states. The South opposed this plan. Another compromise was in order. In the end, Congress received regulatory power over all trade, including the ability to collect tariffs on exported goods. In the South, this raised another red flag regarding the slave trade, as they were concerned about the effect on their economy if tariffs were levied on slaves. The final agreement allowed importing slaves to continue for twenty years without government intervention. Import taxes on slaves were limited, and after the year 1808, Congress could decide whether to allow continued imports of slaves.

Constitution Objections

Once the Constitution was drafted, it was presented for approval by the states. Nine states needed to approve the document for it to become official. However, debate and discussion continued. Major concerns included:
- The lack of a bill of rights to protect individual freedoms.
- States felt too much power was being handed over to the central government.
- Voters wanted more control over their elected representatives.

Discussion about necessary changes to the Constitution divided roughly into two camps: Federalists and Anti-Federalists. Federalists wanted a strong central government. Anti-Federalists wanted to prevent a tyrannical government from developing if a central government held too much power.

Federalist and Anti-Federalist Camps

Major Federalist leaders included Alexander Hamilton, John Jay and James Madison. They wrote a series of letters, called the Federalist Papers, aimed at convincing the states to ratify the Constitution. These were published in New York papers.

Anti-Federalists included Thomas Jefferson and Patrick Henry. They argued against the Constitution as it was originally drafted in arguments called the Anti-Federalist Papers. The final compromise produced a strong central government controlled by checks and balances. A Bill of Rights was also added, becoming the first ten amendments to the Constitution. These amendments protected rights such as freedom of speech, freedom of religion, and other basic rights. Aside from various amendments added throughout the years, the United States Constitution has remained unchanged.

New Government Administration

The individuals who formed the first administration of the new government are as follows:
- George Washington was elected as the first President of the United States in 1789.
- John Adams, who finished second in the election, became the first Vice President.
- Thomas Jefferson was appointed by Washington as Secretary of State.
- Alexander Hamilton was also appointed Secretary of the Treasury.

Alien and Sedition Acts

When John Adams became president, a war was raging between Britain and France. While Adams and the Federalists backed the British, Thomas Jefferson and the Republican Party supported the French. The United States nearly went to war with France during this time period, while France worked to spread its international standing and influence under the leadership of Napoleon Bonaparte. The Alien and Sedition Acts grew out of this conflict, and made it illegal to speak in a hostile fashion against the existing government. They also allowed the president to deport anyone in the U.S. who was not a citizen and who was suspected of treason or treasonous activity.

When Jefferson became the third president in 1800, he repealed these four laws and pardoned anyone who had been convicted under them.

Political Parties

Many in the U.S. were against political parties after seeing the way parties, or factions, functioned in Britain. The factions in Britain were more interested in personal profit than the overall good of the country, and they did not want this to happen in the U.S.

However, the differences of opinion between Thomas Jefferson and Alexander Hamilton led to formation of political parties. Hamilton favored a stronger central government, while Jefferson felt more power should remain with the states. Jefferson was in favor of strict Constitutional interpretation, while Hamilton believed in a more flexible approach. As various others joined the separate camps, Hamilton backers began to term themselves Federalists while those supporting Jefferson became identified as Democratic-Republicans.

Whig Party, Democratic Party, and Republican Party
Thomas Jefferson was elected president in 1800 and again in 1804. The Federalist Party began a decline, and its major figure, Alexander Hamilton, died in a duel with Aaron Burr in 1804. By 1816, the Federalist Party virtually disappeared.

New parties sprang up to take its place. After 1824, the Democratic-Republican Party suffered a split. The Whigs arose, backing John Quincy Adams and industrial growth. The new Democratic Party formed, in opposition to the Whigs, and their candidate, Andrew Jackson, was elected as president in 1828.

By the 1850s, issues regarding slavery led to the formation of the Republican Party, which was anti-slavery, while the Democratic Party of the time, with a larger interest in the South, favored slavery. This Republican/Democrat division formed the basis of today's two-party system.

Marbury vs. Madison

The main duty of the Supreme Court today is judicial review. This power was largely established by Marbury v. Madison. When John Adams was voted out of office in 1800, he worked, during his final days in office, to appoint Federalist judges to Supreme Court positions, knowing Jefferson, his replacement, held opposing views. As late as March 3, the day before Jefferson was to take office, Adams made last-minute appointments referred to as "Midnight Judges." One of the late appointments was William Marbury. The next day, March 4, Jefferson ordered his Secretary of State, James Madison, not to deliver Marbury's commission. This decision was backed by Chief Justice Marshall, who determined that the Judiciary Act of 1789, which granted the power to deliver commissions, was illegal in that it gave the Judicial Branch powers not granted in the Constitution. This case set precedent for the Supreme Court to nullify laws it found to be unconstitutional.

McCulloch vs. Maryland

Judicial review was further exercised by the Supreme Court in McCulloch v Maryland. When Congress chartered a national bank, the Second Bank of the United States, Maryland voted to tax any bank business dealing with banks chartered outside the state, including the federally chartered bank. Andrew McCulloch, an employee of the Second Bank of the US in Baltimore, refused to pay this tax. The resulting lawsuit from the State of Maryland went to the Supreme Court for judgment.

John Marshall, Chief Justice of the Supreme Court, stated that Congress was within its rights to charter a national bank. In addition, the State of Maryland did not have the power to levy a tax on the federal bank or on the federal government in general. In cases where state and federal government collided, precedent was set for the federal government to prevail.

Treaty of Paris

After the Revolutionary War, the Treaty of Paris, which outlined the terms of surrender of the British to the Americans, granted large parcels of land to the U.S. that were occupied by Native Americans. The new government attempted to claim the land, treating the natives as a conquered people. This approached proved unenforceable.

Next, the government tried purchasing the land from the Indians via a series of treaties as the country expanded westward. In practice, however, these treaties were not honored, and Native Americans were simply dislocated and forced to move farther and farther west as American expansion continued, often with military action.

Indian Removal Act of 1830 and the Treaty of New Echota

The Indian Removal Act of 1830 gave the new American government power to form treaties with Native Americans. In theory, America would claim land east of the Mississippi in exchange for land west of the Mississippi, to which the natives would relocate voluntarily. In practice, many tribal leaders were forced into signing the treaties, and relocation at times occurred by force.

The Treaty of New Echota was supposedly a treaty between the US government and Cherokee tribes in Georgia. However, the treaty was not signed by tribal leaders, but rather by a small portion of the represented people. The leaders protested by refusing to be removed, but President, Martin Van Buren, enforced the treaty by sending soldiers. During their forced relocation, more than 4,000 Cherokee Indians died on what became known as the Trail of Tears.

Early Economic Trends

In the Northeast, the economy mostly depended on manufacturing, industry and industrial development. This led to a dichotomy between rich business owners and industrial leaders and the much poorer workers who supported their businesses. The South continued to depend on agriculture, especially large-scale farms or plantations worked mostly by slaves and indentured servants. In the West, where new settlement had begun to develop, the land was largely wild. Growing communities were essentially agricultural; growing crops and

- 43 -

raising livestock. The differences between regions led each to support different interests both politically and economically.

Louisiana Purchase

With tension still high between France and Britain, Napoleon was in need of money to support his continuing war efforts. To secure necessary funds, he decided to sell the Louisiana Territory to the U.S. At the same time President Thomas Jefferson wanted to buy New Orleans, feeling U.S. trade was made vulnerable to both Spain and France at that port. Instead, Napoleon sold him the entire territory for the bargain price of fifteen million dollars. The Louisiana Territory was larger than all the rest of the United States put together, and it eventually became fifteen additional states.

Federalists in Congress were opposed to the purchase. They feared that the Louisiana Purchase would extend slavery, and that further western growth would weaken the power of the northern states.

Early Foreign Policy

The three major ideas driving American foreign policy during its early years are described below:
- Isolationism – the early US government did not intend to establish colonies, though they did plan to grow larger within the bounds of North America.
- No entangling alliances – both George Washington and Thomas Jefferson were opposed to forming any permanent alliances with other countries or becoming involved in other countries' internal issues.
- Nationalism – a positive patriotic feeling about the United States blossomed quickly among its citizens, particularly after the War of 1812, when the U.S. once again defeated Britain. The Industrial Revolution also sparked increased nationalism by allowing even the most far-flung areas of the U.S. to communicate with each other via telegraph and the expanding railroad.

War of 1812

The War of 1812 grew out of the continuing tension between France and Great Britain. Napoleon continued to strive to conquer Britain, while the U.S. continued trade with both countries, but favoring France and the French colonies. Because of what Britain saw as an alliance between America and France, they determined to bring an end to trade between the two nations.

With the British preventing U.S. trade with the French and the French preventing trade with the British, James Madison's presidency introduced acts to regulate international trade. If either Britain or France removed their restrictions, America would not trade with the other. Napoleon acted first, and Madison prohibited trade with England. England saw this as the U.S. formally siding with the French, and war ensued in 1812.

The War of 1812 has been called the Second American Revolution. It established the superiority of the U.S. naval forces and reestablished U.S. independence from Britain and Europe.

The British had two major objections to America's continued trade with France. First, they saw the US as helping France's war effort by providing supplies and goods. Second, the United States had grown into a competitor, taking trade and money away from British ships and tradesmen. In its attempts to end American trade with France, the British put into effect the Orders in Council, which made any and all French-owned ports off-limits to American ships. They also began to seize American ships and conscript their crews, a practice greatly offensive to the U.S.

Military events

Two major naval battles, at Lake Erie and Lake Champlain, kept the British from invading the U.S. via Canada. American attempts to conquer Canadian lands were not successful.

In another memorable British attack, the British invaded Washington DC and burned the White House. Legend has it that Dolly Madison, the First Lady, salvaged the American flag from the fire. On Christmas Eve, 1814, the Treaty of Ghent officially ended the war. However, Andrew Jackson, unaware that the war was over, managed another victory at New Orleans on January 8, 1815. This victory upped American morale and led to a new wave of nationalism and national pride known as the "Era of Good Feelings."

Monroe Doctrine

On December 2, 1823, President Monroe delivered a message to Congress in which he introduced the Monroe Doctrine. In this address, he stated that any attempts by European powers to establish new colonies on the North American continent would be considered interference in American politics. The U.S. would stay out of European matters, and expected Europe to offer America the same courtesy. This approach to foreign policy stated in no uncertain terms that America would not tolerate any new European colonies in the New World, and that events occurring in Europe would no longer influence the policies and doctrines of the U.S.

Lewis and Clark Expedition

The purchase of the Louisiana Territory from France in 1803 more than doubled the size of the United States. President Thomas Jefferson wanted to have the area mapped and explored, since much of the territory was wilderness. He chose Meriwether Lewis and William Clark to head an expedition into the Louisiana Territory. After two years, Lewis and Clark returned, having traveled all the way to the Pacific Ocean. They brought maps, detailed journals, and various types of knowledge and information about the wide expanse of land they had traversed. The Lewis and Clark Expedition opened up the west in the Louisiana Territory and beyond for further exploration and settlement.

Manifest Destiny

In the 1800's, many believed America was destined by God to expand west, bringing as much of the North American continent as possible under the umbrella of U.S. government. With the Northwest Ordinance and the Louisiana Purchase, over half of the continent became American. However, the rapid and relentless expansion brought conflict with the Native Americans, Great Britain, Mexico and Spain. One result of "Manifest Destiny" was the Mexican-American War, which occurred in 1846-1848. By the end of the war, Texas, California and a large portion of what is now the American Southwest joined the growing nation. Conflict also arose over the Oregon country, shared by the US and Britain. In 1846, President James Polk resolved this problem by compromising with Britain, establishing a U.S. boundary south of the 49th parallel.

Mexican-American War

Spain had held colonial interests in America since the 1540s—earlier even than Great Britain. In 1821, Mexico revolted against Spain and became a free nation. Likewise, this was followed by Texas, who after an 1836 revolution declared its independence. In 1844, the Democrats pressed President Tyler to annex Texas. Unlike his predecessor, Andrew Jackson, Tyler agreed to admit Texas into the Union. In 1845, Texas became a state.

During Mexico's war for independence, they had incurred $4.5 million in war debts to the U.S. Polk offered to forgive the debts in return for New Mexico and Upper California, but Mexico refused. In 1846, war was declared in response to a Mexican attack on American troops along the southern border of Texas. Additional conflict arose in Congress over the Wilmot Proviso, which stated that any territory the U.S. acquired from Mexico should be legally open to slavery. The war ended in 1848.

Gadsden Purchase and the 1853 post-war treaty with Mexico

After the Mexican-American war, a second treaty in 1853 determined hundreds of miles of America's southwest borders. In 1854, the Gadsden Purchase was finalized, providing even more territory to aid in the building of the transcontinental railroad. This purchase added what would eventually become the southernmost regions of Arizona and New Mexico to the growing nation. The modern outline of the United States was by this time nearly complete.

American System

Spurred by the trade conflicts of the War of 1812, and supported by Henry Clay and others, the American System set up tariffs to help protect American interests from competition with products from overseas. Reducing competition led to growth in employment and an overall increase in American industry. The higher tariffs also provided funds for the government to pay for various improvements. Congress passed high tariffs in 1816 and also chartered a federal bank. The Second Bank of the United States was given the job of regulating America's money supply.

Jacksonian Democracy

Jacksonian Democracy is largely seen as a shift from politics favoring the wealthy to politics favoring the common man. All free white males were given the right to vote, not just property owners, as had been the case previously. Jackson's approach favored the patronage system, Laissez faire economics, and relocation of the Indian tribes from the Southeast portion of the country. Jackson opposed the formation of a federal bank and allowed the Second Band of the United States to collapse by vetoing a bill to renew the charter. Jackson also faced the challenge of the "null and void" or nullification theory when South Carolina claimed that it could ignore or nullify any federal law it considered unconstitutional. Jackson sent troops to the state to enforce the protested tariff laws, and a compromise engineered by Henry Clay in 1833 settled the matter for the time being.

Conflict Between North and South

The conflict between North and South coalesced around the issue of slavery, but other elements contributed to the growing disagreement. Though most farmers in the South worked small farms with little or no slave labor, the huge plantations run by the South's rich depended on slaves or indentured servants to remain profitable. They had also become more dependent on cotton, with slave populations growing in concert with the rapid increase in cotton production. In the North, a more diverse agricultural economy and the growth of industry made slaves rarer. The abolitionist movement grew steadily, with Harriet Beecher Stowe's *Uncle Tom's Cabin* giving many an idea to rally around. A collection of anti-slavery organizations formed, with many actively working to free slaves in the South, often bringing them North.

Anti-Slavery Organizations

Five anti-slavery organizations and their significance are:
- American Colonization Society—protestant churches formed this group, aimed at returning black slaves to Africa. Former slaves subsequently formed Liberia, but the colony did not do well, as the region was not well-suited for agriculture.
- American Anti-Slavery Society—William Lloyd Garrison, a Quaker, was the major force behind this group and its newspaper, *The Liberator.*
- Female Anti-Slavery Society—a women-only group formed by Margaretta Forten because women were not allowed to join the Anti-Slavery Society formed by her father.
- Anti-Slavery Convention of American Women—This group continued meeting even after pro-slavery factions burned down their original meeting place.
- Female Vigilant Society—an organization that raised funds to help the Underground Railroad, as well as slave refugees.

Educational Attitudes

Horace Mann, among others, felt that public schooling could help children become better citizens, keep them away from crime, prevent poverty, and help American society become more unified. His *Common School Journal* brought his ideas of the importance of education into the public consciousness. Increased literacy led to increased awareness of current events, Western expansion, and other major developments of the time period. Public interest and participation in the arts and literature also increased. By the end of the 19th century, all children had access to a free public elementary education.

Transportation

As America expanded its borders, it also developed new technology to travel the rapidly growing country. Roads and railroads traversed the nation, with the Transcontinental Railroad eventually allowing travel from one coast to the other. Canals and steamboats simplified water travel and made shipping easier and less expensive. The Erie Canal (1825) connected the Great Lakes with the Hudson River. Other canals connected other major water ways, further facilitating transportation and the shipment of goods.

With growing numbers of settlers moving into the West, wagon trails developed, including the Oregon Trail, California Trail and the Santa Fe Trail. The most common vehicles seen along these westbound trails were covered wagons, also known as prairie schooners.

Industrial Activity and Major Inventions

During the eighteenth century, goods were often manufactured in houses or small shops. With increased technology allowing for the use of machines, factories began to develop. In factories a large volume of salable goods could be produced in a much shorter amount of time. Many Americans, including increasing numbers of immigrants, found jobs in these factories, which were in constant need of labor. Another major invention was the cotton gin, which significantly decreased the processing time of cotton and was a major factor in the rapid expansion of cotton production in the South.

Labor Movements in the 1800s

In 1751, a group of bakers held a protest in which they stopped baking bread. This was technically the first American labor strike. In the 1830s and 1840s, labor movements began in earnest. Boston's masons, carpenters and stoneworkers protested the length of the workday, fighting to reduce it to ten hours. In 1844, a group of women in the textile industry also fought to reduce their workday to ten hours, forming the Lowell Female Labor Reform Association. Many other protests occurred and organizations developed through this time period with the same goal in mind.

Second Great Awakening

Led by Protestant evangelical leaders, the Second Great Awakening occurred between 1800 and 1830. Several missionary groups grew out of the movement, including the American Home Missionary Society, which formed in 1826. The ideas behind the Second Great Awakening focused on personal responsibility, both as an individual and in response to injustice and suffering. The American Bible Society and the American Tract Society provided literature, while various traveling preachers spread the word. New denominations arose, including the Latter Day Saints and Seventh-Day Adventists.

Another movement associated with the Second Great Awakening was the temperance movement, focused on ending the production and use of alcohol. One major organization behind the temperance movement was the Society for the Promotion of Temperance, formed in 1826 in Boston, Massachusetts.

Women's Rights Movement

The women's rights movement began in the 1840s with leaders including Elizabeth Cady Stanton, Ernestine Rose and Lucretia Mott. Later, in 1869, the National Woman Suffrage Association, fighting for women's right to vote, came into being. It was led by Susan B. Anthony, Ernestine Rose and Elizabeth Cady Stanton.

In 1848 in Seneca Falls, the first women's rights convention was held, with about three hundred attendees. The Seneca Falls Convention brought to the floor the issue that women could not vote or run for office. The convention produced a "Declaration of Sentiments" which outlined a plan for women to attain the rights they deserved. Frederick

Douglass supported the women's rights movement, as well as the abolition movement. In fact, women's rights and abolition movements often went hand-in-hand through this time period.

Missouri Compromise

By 1819, the United States had developed a tenuous balance between slave and free states, with exactly twenty-two senators in Congress from each faction. However, Missouri was ready to join the union as a state. As a slave state, it would tip the balance in Congress. To prevent this imbalance, the Missouri Compromise brought the northern part of Massachusetts into the union as Maine, established as a free state. Maine's admission balanced the admission of Missouri as a slave state, maintaining the status quo. In addition, the remaining portion of the Louisiana Purchase was to remain free north of latitude 36° 30'. Since cotton did not grow well this far north, this limitation was acceptable to congressmen representing the slave states.

However, the proposed Missouri constitution presented a problem, as it outlawed immigration of free blacks into the state. Another compromise was in order, this time proposed by Henry Clay. Clay earned his title of the Great Compromiser by stating that the U.S. Constitution overruled Missouri's.

Popular Sovereignty and the Compromise of 1850

In addition to the pro-slavery and anti-slavery factions, a third group rose who felt that each individual state should decide whether to allow or permit slavery within its borders. This idea was referred to as popular sovereignty.

When California applied to join the union in 1849, the balance of congressional power was again threatened. The Compromise of 1850 introduced a group of laws meant to bring an end to the conflict.

These laws included:
- California being admitted as a free state.
- Slave trade in Washington, D.C. being outlawed.
- An increase in efforts to capture escaped slaves.
- New Mexico and Utah territories would decide individually whether or not to allow slavery.

In spite of these measures, debate raged each time a new state prepared to enter the union.

Kansas-Nebraska Act

With the creation of the Kansas and Nebraska territories in 1854, another debate began. Congress allowed popular sovereignty in these territories, but slavery opponents argued that the Missouri Compromise had already made slavery illegal in this region. In Kansas, two separate governments arose, one pro- and one anti-slavery. Conflict between the two factions rose to violence, leading Kansas to gain the nickname of "Bleeding Kansas."

Dred Scott Decision

Abolitionist factions coalesced around the case of Dred Scott, using his case to test the country's laws regarding slavery. Scott, a slave, had been taken by his owner from Missouri, which was a slave state. He then traveled to Illinois, a free state, then on to the Minnesota Territory, also free based on the Missouri Compromise. Then, he returned to Missouri. The owner subsequently died. Abolitionists took Scott's case to court, stating that Scott was no longer a slave but free, since he had lived in free territory. The case went to the Supreme Court.

The Supreme Court stated that, because Scott, as a slave, was not a U.S. citizen, his time in free states did not change his status. He also did not have the right to sue. In addition, the Court determined that the Missouri Compromise was unconstitutional, saying Congress had overstepped its bounds by outlawing slavery in the territories.

Harper's Ferry and John Brown

John Brown, an abolitionist, had participated in several anti-slavery actions, including killing five pro-slavery men in retaliation, after Lawrence, Kansas, an anti-slavery town, was sacked. He and other abolitionists also banded together to pool their funds and build a runaway slave colony.
In 1859, Brown seized a federal arsenal in Harper's Ferry, located in what is now West Virginia. Brown intended to seize guns and ammunition and lead a slave rebellion. Robert E. Lee captured Brown and 22 followers, who were subsequently tried and hanged. While Northerners took the executions as an indication that the government supported slavery, Southerners were of the opinion that most of the North supported Brown and were, in general, anti-slavery.

1860 Election

The 1860 Presidential candidates represented four different parties, each with a different opinion on slavery.
- John Breckenridge, representing the Southern Democrats, was pro-slavery.
- Abraham Lincoln, of the Republican Party, was anti-slavery.
- Stephen Douglas, of the Northern Democrats, felt that the issue should be determined locally, on a state-by-state basis.
- John Bell, of the Constitutional Union Party, focused primarily on keeping the Union intact.

In the end, Abraham Lincoln won both the popular and electoral election. Southern states, who had sworn to secede from the Union if Lincoln was elected did so, led by South Carolina. Shortly thereafter, the Civil War began when shots were fired on Fort Sumter in Charleston.

Advantages of the North and South in the Civil War

The Northern states had significant advantages, including:
- Larger population. The North consisted of 24 states to the South's 11.
- Better transportation and finances. With railroads primarily in the North, supply chains were much more dependable, as was trade coming from overseas.
- More raw materials. The North held the majority of America's gold, as well as iron, copper and other minerals vital to wartime.

The South's advantages included:
- Better-trained military officers. Many of the Southern officers were West Point trained and had commanded in the Mexican and Indian wars.
- More familiar with weapons. The climate and lifestyle of the South meant most of the people were well versed in both guns and horses. The industrial North had less extensive experience
- Defensive position. The South felt victory was guaranteed, since they were protecting their own lands, while the North would be invading.
- Well-defined goals. The South was fighting an ideological war to be allowed to govern themselves and preserve their way of life.

Emancipation Proclamation

The Emancipation Proclamation, issued by President Lincoln in 1862, freed all slaves in Confederate States that did not return to the Union by the beginning of the year. While the original proclamation did not free any slaves actually under Union control, it did set a precedent for the emancipation of slaves as the war progressed.

The Emancipation Proclamation worked in the Union's favor as many freed slaves and other black troops joined the Union Army. Almost 200,000 blacks fought in the Union army, and over 10,000 served in the navy. By the end of the war, over 4 million slaves had been freed, and in 1865 slavery was banned by Constitutional amendment.

Civil War Events

Six major events of the Civil War and their outcomes or significance are as follows:
- The Battle of Bull Run, July 21, 1861. The First Battle of Bull Run, was the first major land battle of the war. Observers, expecting to enjoy an entertaining skirmish, set up picnics nearby. Instead, they found themselves witness to a bloodbath. Union forces were defeated, and the battle set the course of the Civil War as long, bloody and costly.
- The Capture of Fort Henry by Ulysses S. Grant. This battle in February of 1862 marked the Union's first major victory.
- The Battle of Gettysburg, July 1-3, 1863. Often seen as the turning point of the war, Gettysburg also saw the largest number of casualties of the war, with over 50,000 dead. Robert E. Lee was defeated, and the Confederate army, significantly crippled, withdrew.
- The Overland Campaign, 1864. Grant, now in command of all the Union armies, led this high casualty campaign that eventually positioned the Union for victory.
- Sherman's March to the Sea. William Tecumseh Sherman, in May of 1864, conquered Atlanta. He then continued to Savannah, destroying indiscriminately as he went.
- Following Lee's defeat at the Appomattox Courthouse, General Grant accepted Lee's surrender in the home of Wilmer McLean, Appomattox, Virginia on April 9, 1865.

Lincoln's Assassination

The Civil War ended with the surrender of the South on April 9, 1865. Five days later, Lincoln and his wife, Mary, attended the play *Our American Cousin* at the Ford Theater. John Wilkes Booth, unaware that the war was over, performed his part in a conspiracy to aid the

Confederacy by shooting Lincoln in the back of the head. Booth was tracked down and killed by Union soldiers 12 days later. Lincoln, carried from the theater to a nearby house, died the next morning.

Reconstruction and the Freedmen's Bureau

In the aftermath of the Civil War, the South was left in chaos. From 1865 to 1877, government on all levels worked to help restore order to the South, ensure civil rights to the freed slaves, and bring the Confederate states back into the Union.
In 1866, Congress passed the Reconstruction Acts, putting former Confederate states under military rule.

The Freedmen's Bureau was formed to help freedmen and give assistance to whites in the South who needed basic necessities like food and clothing. Many in the South felt the Freedmen's Bureau worked to set freed slaves against their former owners. The Bureau was intended to help former slaves become self-sufficient, and to keep them from falling prey to those who would take advantage of them.

Radical and Moderate Republicans

The Radical Republicans wished to treat the South quite harshly after the war. Thaddeus Stephens, the House Leader, suggested that the Confederate States be treated as if they were territories again, with ten years of military rule and territorial government before they would be readmitted. They also wanted to give all black men the right to vote. Former Confederate soldiers would be required to swear they had not fought against the Union in order to be granted full rights as American citizens.

By contrast, the moderate Republicans wanted only black men who were literate or who had served as Union troops to be able to vote. All Confederate soldiers except troop leaders would also be able to vote. Before his death, Lincoln had favored a more moderate approach to Reconstruction, hoping this approach might bring some states back into the Union before the end of the war.

Black Codes and the Civil Rights Bill

The Black Codes were proposed to control freed slaves. They would not be allowed to bear arms, assemble, serve on juries, or testify against whites. Schools would be segregated, and unemployed blacks could be arrested and forced to work.

The Civil Rights bill countered these codes, providing much wider rights for the freed slaves.

Andrew Johnson, who became president after Lincoln's death, supported the Black Codes, and vetoed the Civil Rights bill. Congress overrode his veto and impeached Johnson, the culmination of tensions between Congress and the president. He came within a single vote of being convicted.

Thirteenth, Fourteenth and Fifteenth Amendments

The Thirteenth, Fourteenth and Fifteenth Amendments, all passed shortly after the end of the Civil War, are described below:

- The Thirteenth Amendment was passed on December 18, 1865. This amendment prohibited slavery in the United States.
- The Fourteenth Amendment overturned the Dred Scott decision, and was ratified July 9, 1868. American citizenship was redefined, with all citizens guaranteed equal legal protection by all states. It also guaranteed citizens the right to file a lawsuit or serve on a jury.
- The Fifteenth Amendment was ratified February 3, 1870. It states that no citizen of the United States can be denied the right to vote based on race, color, or previous status as a slave.

Reconstruction

The three phases of Reconstruction are:
- Presidential Reconstruction – largely driven by President Andrew Johnson's policies, the Presidential phase of Reconstruction was lenient on the South and allowed continued discrimination against and control over blacks.
- Congressional Reconstruction – Congress, controlled largely by Radical Republicans, took a different stance, providing a wider range of civil rights for blacks and greater control over Southern government. Congressional Reconstruction is marked by military control of the former Confederate States.
- Redemption – Gradually, the Confederate states were readmitted into the union. During this time, white Democrats took over the government of most of the South. Troops finally departed the South in 1877.

Carpetbaggers and Scalawags

The chaos in the south attracted a number of people seeking to fill the power vacuums and take advantage of the economic disruption. Scalawags were southern Whites who aligned with Freedmen to take over local governments. Many in the South who could have filled political offices refused to take the necessary oath required to grant them the right to vote, leaving many opportunities for Scalawags and others. Carpetbaggers were northerners who traveled to the South for various reasons. Some provided assistance, while others sought to make money or to acquire political power during this chaotic period.

Transcontinental Railroad

In 1869, the Union Pacific Railroad completed the first section of a planned transcontinental railroad. This section went from Omaha, Nebraska to Sacramento, California. With the rise of the railroad, products were much more easily transported across country. While this was positive overall for industry throughout the country, it was often damaging to family farmers, who found themselves paying high shipping costs for smaller supply orders while larger companies received major discounts. Ninety percent of the workers constructing the railroad were Chinese, working in very dangerous conditions for very low pay.

Immigrations Acts

In 1870, the Naturalization Act put limits on U.S. citizenship, allowing full citizenship only to whites and those of African descent. The Chinese Exclusion Act of 1882 put limits on Chinese immigration. The Immigration Act of 1882 taxed immigrants, charging fifty cents per person. These funds helped pay administrative costs for regulating immigration. Ellis Island opened in 1892 as a processing center those arriving in New York. 1921 saw the Emergency Quota Act passed, also known as the Johnson Quota Act, which severely limited the number of immigrants allowed into the country.

Agriculture Improvements

Technological advancements
During the mid 1800s, irrigation techniques improved significantly. Advances occurred in cultivation and breeding, as well as fertilizer use and crop rotation. In the Great Plains, also known as the Great American Desert, the dense soil was finally cultivated with steel plows. In 1892, gasoline-powered tractors arrived, and were widely used by 1900. Other advancements in agriculture's tool set included barbed wire fences, combines, silos, deep-water wells, and the cream separator.

Government actions
Four major actions by the government that helped improve agriculture for the U.S. in the nineteenth century are as follows:
- The Department of Agriculture came into being in 1862, working for the interests of farmers and ranchers across the country.
- The Morrill Land-Grant Acts were passed in 1862, allowing land-grant colleges.
- In conjunction with land-grant colleges, the Hatch Act of 1887 brought agriculture experimental stations into the picture, helping discover new farming techniques.
- In 1914, the Smith-Lever Act provided cooperative programs to help educate people about food, home economics, community development and agriculture. Related agriculture extension programs helped farmers increase crop production to feed the rapidly growing nation.

Inventions

Major inventors from the 1800s and their inventions are:
- Alexander Graham Bell—the telephone
- Orville and Wilbur Wright—the airplane
- Richard Gatling—the machine gun
- Walter Hunt, Elias Howe and Isaac Singer—the sewing machine
- Nikola Tesla—alternating current
- George Eastman—the camera
- Thomas Edison—light bulbs, motion pictures, the phonograph
- Samuel Morse—the telegraph
- Charles Goodyear—vulcanized rubber
- Cyrus McCormick—the reaper
- George Westinghouse—the transformer, the air brake

This was an active period for invention, with about 700,000 patents registered between 1860 and 1900.

United States History from 1877 to the Present

Gilded Age

The time period from the end of the Civil War to the beginning of the First World War is often referred to as the Gilded Age, or the Second Industrial Revolution. The U.S. was changing from an agriculturally based economy to an industrial economy, with rapid growth accompanying the shift. In addition, the country itself was expanding, spreading into the seemingly unlimited West.

This time period saw the beginning of banks, department stores, chain stores, and trusts—all familiar features of our modern-day landscape. Cities also grew rapidly, and large numbers of immigrants arrived in the country, swelling the urban ranks.

Populist Party

A major recession struck the United States during the 1890s, with crop prices falling dramatically. Drought compounded the problems, leaving many American farmers in crippling debt. The Farmers Alliance formed, drawing the rural poor into a single political entity.

Recession also affected the more industrial parts of the country. The Knights of Labor, formed in 1869 by Uriah Stephens, was able to unite workers into a union to protect their rights. Dissatisfied by views espoused by industrialists, these two groups, the Farmers Alliance and the Knights of Labor, joined to form the Populist Party. Some of the elements of the party's platform included:
- National currency
- Income tax
- Government ownership of railroads, telegraph and telephone systems
- Secret ballot for voting
- Immigration restriction
- Term limits for President and Vice-President

The Populist Party was in favor of decreasing elitism and making the voice of the common man more easily heard in the political process.

Labor Movement

The first large, well-organized strike occurred in 1892. Called the Homestead Strike, it occurred when the Amalgamated Association of Iron and Steel Works struck against the Carnegie Steel Company. Gunfire ensued, and Carnegie was able to eliminate the plant's union. In 1894, workers, led by Eugene Debs, initiated the Pullman Strike after the Pullman Palace Car Co. cut their wages by 28 percent. President Grover Cleveland called in troops to break up the strike on the grounds that it interfered with mail delivery. Mary Harris Jones, also known as Mother Jones, organized the Children's Crusade to protest child labor. A protest march proceeded to the home of President Theodore Roosevelt in 1902. Jones also worked with the United Mine Workers of America, and helped found the Industrial Workers of the World.

Panic of 1893

Far from a U.S.-centric event, the Panic of 1893 was an economic crisis that affected most of the globe. As a response to the Panic, President Grover Cleveland repealed the Sherman Silver Purchase Act, afraid it had caused the downturn rather than boosting the economy as intended. The Panic led to bankruptcies, with railroads going under and factory unemployment rising as high as 25 percent. In the end, the Republican Party regained power due to the economic crisis.

Progressive Era

From the 1890s to the end of the First World War, Progressives set forth an ideology that drove many levels of society and politics. The Progressives were in favor of workers' rights and safety, and wanted measures taken against waste and corruption. They felt science could help improve society, and that the government could—and should—provide answers to a variety of social problems. Progressives came from a wide variety of backgrounds, but were united in their desire to improve society.

Muckrakers
"Muckrakers" was a term used to identify aggressive investigative journalists who brought to light scandals, corruption, and many other wrongs being perpetrated in late nineteenth century society. Among these intrepid writers were:
- Ida Tarbell—he exposed the Standard Oil Trust.
- Jacob Riis—a photographer, he helped improve the lot of the poor in New York.
- Lincoln Steffens—he worked to expose political corruption.
- Upton Sinclair—his book *The Jungle* led to reforms in the meat packing industry.

Through the work of these journalists, many new policies came into being, including workmen's compensation, child labor laws, and trust-busting.

Sixteenth, Seventeenth, Eighteenth and Nineteenth Amendments
The early twentieth century saw several amendments made to the U.S. Constitution. These included:
- Sixteenth Amendment, 1913 established a graduated income tax.
- Seventeenth Amendment, 1913 allowed direct election of Senators.
- Eighteenth Amendment, 1919 prohibited the sale, production and importation of alcohol. This amendment was later repealed by the Twenty-first Amendment.
- Nineteenth Amendment, 1920 gave women the right to vote.

These amendments largely grew out of the Progressive Era, as many citizens worked to improve American society.

Federal Trade Commission and elimination of trusts
Muckrakers such as Ida Tarbell and Lincoln Steffens brought to light the damaging trend of trusts—huge corporations working to monopolize areas of commerce and so control prices and distribution. The Sherman Act and the Clayton Antitrust Act set out guidelines for competition among corporations and set out to eliminate these trusts. The Federal Trade

Commission was formed in order to enforce antitrust measures and ensure companies were operated fairly and did not create controlling monopolies.

Native Americans

America's westward expansion led to conflict and violent confrontations with Native Americans such as the Battle of Little Bighorn. In 1876, the American government ordered all Indians to relocate to reservations. Lack of compliance led to the Dawes Act in 1887, which ordered assimilation rather than separation. This act remained in effect until 1934. Reformers also forced Indian children to attend Indian Boarding Schools, where they were not allowed to speak their native language and were forced to accept Christianity. Children were often abused in these schools, and were indoctrinated to abandon their identity as Native Americans.

In 1890, the massacre at Wounded Knee, accompanied by Geronimo's surrender, led the Native Americans to work to preserve their culture rather than fight for their lands.

Native Americans in wartime
The Spanish-American war, 1898-1902, saw a number of Native Americans serving with Teddy Roosevelt in the Rough Riders. Apache scouts accompanied General John J. Pershing to Mexico, hoping to find Pancho Villa. More than 17,000 Native Americans were drafted into service for World War I, though at the time they were not considered as legal citizens. In 1924, Indians were finally granted official citizenship by the Indian Citizenship Act. After decades of relocation, forced assimilation and outright genocide the number of Native Americans in the U.S. has greatly declined. Though many Native Americans have chosen—or have been forced—to assimilate, about 300 reservations exist today, with most of their inhabitants living in abject poverty.

Spanish-American War

Spain had controlled Cuba since the fifteenth century. Over the centuries, the Spanish had quashed a variety of revolts. In 1886, slavery ended in Cuba, and another revolt was rising.

In the meantime, the US had expressed interest in Cuba, offering Spain $130 million for the island in 1853, during Franklin Pierce's presidency. In 1898, the Cuban revolt was underway. In spite of various factions supporting the Cubans, the US President, William McKinley, refused to recognize the rebellion, preferring negotiation over involvement in war. Then The Maine, a US battleship in Havana Harbor, was blown up, costing nearly 300 lives. The US declared war two months later, and the war ended four months later with a Spanish surrender.

Panama Canal

Initial work began on the Panama Canal in 1880, though the idea had been discussed since the 1500s. The Canal greatly reduces the length and time needed to sail from one ocean to the other by connecting the Atlantic to the Pacific through the Isthmus of Panama, which joins South America to North America. Before the Canal was built, travelers had to sail all the way around South America to reach the West Coast of the US. The French began the work in 1880, after successfully completing the Suez Canal, connecting the Mediterranean Sea to the Red Sea. However, their efforts quickly fell apart. The US moved in to take over, completing the complex canal in 1914. The Panama Canal was constructed as a lock-and-lake canal, with ships actually lifted on locks to travel from one lake to another over the rugged, mountainous terrain. In order to maintain control of the Canal Zone, the US assisted Panama in its battle for independence from Columbia.

Roosevelt's "Big Stick Diplomacy"

Theodore Roosevelt's famous quote, "Speak softly and carry a big stick," is supposedly of African origins, at least according to Roosevelt. He used this proverb to justify expanded involvement in foreign affairs during his tenure as President. The US military was deployed to protect American interests in Latin America. Roosevelt also worked to maintain an equal or greater influence in Latin America than those held by European interests. As a result, the US Navy grew larger, and the US generally became more involved in foreign affairs. Roosevelt felt that if any country was left vulnerable to control by Europe, due to economic issues or political instability, the US had not only a right to intervene, but was obligated to do so. This led to US involvement in Cuba, Nicaragua, Haiti and the Dominican Republic over several decades leading into the First and Second World Wars.

William Howard Taft's "Dollar Diplomacy"

During William Howard Taft's presidency, Taft instituted "Dollar Diplomacy." This approach was used as a description of American efforts to influence Latin America and East Asia through economic rather than military means. Taft saw past efforts in these areas to be political and warlike, while his efforts focused on peaceful economic goals. His justification of the policy was to protect the Panama Canal, which was vital to US trade interests.

In spite of Taft's assurance that Dollar Diplomacy was a peaceful approach, many interventions proved violent. During Latin American revolts, such as those in Nicaragua, the US sent troops to settle the revolutions. Afterwards, bankers moved in to help support the new leaders through loans. Dollar Diplomacy continued until 1913, when Woodrow Wilson was elected President.

Woodrow Wilson's "Moral Diplomacy"

Turning away from Taft's "Dollar Diplomacy", Wilson instituted a foreign policy he referred to as "moral diplomacy." This approach still influences American foreign policy today. Wilson felt that representative government and democracy in all countries would lead to worldwide stability. Democratic governments, he felt, would be less likely to threaten American interests. He also saw the US and Great Britain as the great role models in this area, as well as champions of world peace and self-government. Free trade and international commerce would allow the US to speak out regarding world events. Main elements of Wilson's policies included:
- Maintaining a strong military
- Promoting democracy throughout the world
- Expanding international trade to boost the American economy

World War I

The First World War occurred from 1914 to 1918 and was fought largely in Europe. Triggered by the assassination of Austrian Archduke Francis Ferdinand, the war rapidly escalated. At the beginning of the conflict, Woodrow Wilson declared the US neutral. Major events influencing US involvement included:

- Sinking of the Lusitania - The British passenger liner RMS Lusitania was sunk by a German U-boat in 1915. Among the 1,000 civilian victims were 100 Americans. Outraged by this act, many Americans began to push for US involvement in the war, using the Lusitania as a rallying cry.
- German U-boat aggression - Wilson continued to keep the US out of the war, with his 1916 reelection slogan, "He kept us out of war." While he continued to work toward an end of the war, German U-boats began to indiscriminately attack American and Canadian merchant ships carrying supplies to Germany's enemies in Europe.
- Zimmerman Note - The final event that brought the US into World War I was the interception of the Zimmerman Note. In this telegram, Germany communicated with the Mexican government its intentions to invade the US with Mexico's assistance.

American railroads came under government control in December 1917. The widespread system was consolidated into a single system, with each region assigned a director. This greatly increased the efficiency of the railroad system, allowing the railroads to supply both domestic and military needs. Control returned to private ownership in 1920. In 1918, telegraph, telephone and cable services also came under Federal control, to be returned to private management the next year. The American Red Cross supported the war effort by knitting clothes for Army and Navy troops. They also helped supply hospital and refugee clothing and surgical dressings. Over eight million people participated in this effort. To generate wartime funds, the US government sold Liberty Bonds. In four issues, they sold nearly $25 billion—more than one fifth of Americans purchased them. After the war, Liberty Bonds were replaced with Victory Bonds.

Wilson's Fourteen Points

President Woodrow Wilson proposed Fourteen Points as the basis for a peace settlement to end the war. Presented to the US Congress in January 1918, the Fourteen Points included:

- Five points outlining general ideals
- Eight points to resolve immediate problems of political and territorial nature
- One point proposing an organization of nations with the intent of maintaining world peace

In November of that same year, Germany agreed to an armistice, assuming the final treaty would be based on the Fourteen Points. However, during the peace conference in Paris 1919, there was much disagreement, leading to a final agreement that punished Germany and the other Central Powers much more than originally intended. Henry Cabot Lodge, who had become the Foreign Relations Committee chairman in 1918, wanted an unconditional surrender from Germany. A League of Nations was included in the Treaty of Versailles at Wilson's insistence. The Senate rejected the Treaty of Versailles, and in the end Wilson refused to concede to Lodge's demands. As a result, the US did not join the League of Nations.

1920's

The post-war '20s saw many Americans moving from the farm to the city, with growing prosperity in the US. The Roaring Twenties, or the Jazz Age, was driven largely by growth in the automobile and entertainment industries. Individuals like Charles Lindbergh, the first aviator to make a solo flight cross the Atlantic Ocean, added to the American admiration of individual accomplishment. Telephone lines, distribution of electricity, highways, the radio, and other inventions brought great changes to everyday life.

Cultural movements influenced or driven by African Americans

The Harlem Renaissance saw a number of African American artists settling in Harlem, New York City. This community produced a number of well-known artists and writers, including Langston Hughes, Nella Larson, Zora Neale Hurston, Claude McKay, Countee Cullen and Jean Toomer. The growth of jazz, also largely driven by African Americans, defined the Jazz Age. Its unconventional, improvisational style matched the growing sense of optimism and exploration of the decade. Originating as an offshoot of the blues, jazz began in New Orleans. Some significant jazz musicians were Duke Ellington, Louis Armstrong and Jelly Roll Morton. Big Band and Swing Jazz also developed in the 1920s. Well-known musicians of this movement included Bing Crosby, Frank Sinatra, Count Basie, Benny Goodman, Billie Holiday, Ella Fitzgerald and The Dorsey Brothers.

National Origins Act of 1924

The National Origins Act (Johnson-Reed Act) placed limitations on immigration. The number of immigrants allowed into the US was based on the population of each nationality of immigrants who were living in the country in 1890. Only two percent of each nationality's 1890 population numbers were allowed to immigrate. This led to great disparities between immigrants from various nations, and Asian immigration was not allowed at all. Some of the impetus behind the Johnson-Reed Act came as a result of paranoia following the Russian Revolution. Fear of communist influences in the US led to a general fear of immigrants.

Red Scare

World War I created many jobs, but after the war ended these jobs disappeared, leaving many unemployed. In the wake of these employment changes the International Workers of the World and the Socialist Party, headed by Eugene Debs, became more and more visible. Workers initiated strikes in an attempt to regain the favorable working conditions that had been put into place before the war. Unfortunately, many of these strikes became violent, and the actions were blamed on "Reds," or Communists, for trying to spread their views into America. With the Bolshevik Revolution being recent news in Russia, many Americans feared a similar revolution might occur here. The Red Scare ensued, with many individuals jailed for supposedly holding communist, anarchist or socialist beliefs.

African American Civil Rights

Marcus Garvey founded the Universal Negro Improvement Association, which became a large and active organization focused on building black nationalism. In 1911, the National Association for the Advancement of Colored People (NAACP) came into being, working to defeat Jim Crow laws. The NAACP also helped prevent racial segregation from becoming federal law, fought against lynchings, helped black soldiers in WWI become officers, and helped defend the Scottsboro Boys, who were unjustly accused of rape.

Ku Klux Klan

In 1866, Confederate Army veterans came together to fight against Reconstruction in the South, forming a group called the Ku Klux Klan (KKK). With white supremacist beliefs, including anti-Semitism, nativism, anti-Catholicism, and overt racism, this organization relied heavily on violence to get its message across. In 1915, they grew again in power, using a film called *The Birth of a Nation*, by D.W. Griffith, to spread their ideas. In the 1920s, the reach of the KKK spread far into the North and Midwest, and members controlled a number of state governments. Its membership and power began to decline during the Great Depression, but experienced a major resurgence later.

American Civil Liberties Union

The American Civil Liberties Union (ACLU), founded in 1920, grew from the American Union Against Militarism. This former organization helped conscientious objectors avoid going to war during WWI, and also helped those being prosecuted under the Espionage Act (1917) and the Sedition Act (1918), many of whom were immigrants. Their major goals were to protect immigrants and other citizens who were threatened with prosecution for their political beliefs, and to support labor unions, which were also under threat by the government during the Red Scare.

Anti-Defamation League

In 1913, the Anti-Defamation League was formed to prevent anti-Semitic behavior and practices. Its actions also worked to prevent all forms of racism, and to prevent individuals from being discriminated against for any reason involving their race. They spoke against the Ku Klux Klan, as well as other racist or anti-Semitic organizations. This organization still exists, and still works to fight discrimination against minorities of all kinds.

Great Depression

The Great Depression, which began in 1929 with the Stock Market Crash, grew out of several factors that had developed over the previous years including:
- Growing economic disparity between the rich and middle-class, with the rich amassing wealth much more quickly than the lower classes
- Disparity in economic distribution in industries
- Growing use of credit, leading to an inflated demand for some goods
- Government support of new industries rather than providing additional support for agriculture
- Risky stock market investments, leading to the stock market crash

Additional factors contributing to the Depression also included the Labor Day Hurricane in the Florida Keys (1935) and the Great Hurricane of 1938, in Long Island, along with the Dust Bowl in the Great Plains, which destroyed crops and resulted in the displacement of as many as 2.5 million people.

Roosevelt Administration

Roosevelt's "New Deal"
Franklin D. Roosevelt was elected president in 1932 with his promise of a "New Deal" for Americans. His goals were to provide government work programs to provide jobs, wages and relief to numerous workers throughout the beleaguered US. Congress gave Roosevelt almost free rein to produce relief legislation. The goals of this legislation were:
- Relief: Accomplished largely by creating jobs
- Recovery: Stimulate the economy through the National Recovery Administration
- Reform: Pass legislation to prevent future similar economic crashes

The Roosevelt Administration also passed legislation regarding ecological issues, including the Soil Conservation Service, aimed at preventing another Dust Bowl.

Roosevelt's "alphabet organizations"
So-called alphabet organizations set up during Roosevelt's administration included:
- Civilian Conservation Corps (CCC)—provided jobs in the forestry service
- Agricultural Adjustment Administration (AAA)—increased agricultural income by adjusting both production and prices.
- Tennessee Valley Authority (TVA)—organized projects to build dams in the Tennessee River for flood control and production of electricity, resulting in increased productivity for industries in the area, and easier navigation of the Tennessee River
- Public Works Administration (PWA) and Civil Works Administration (CWA)—initiated over 34,000 projects, providing employment
- Works Progress Administration (WPA)—helped unemployed persons to secure employment on government work projects or elsewhere

Actions taken to prevent future crashes and stabilize the economy
The Roosevelt administration passed several laws and established several institutions to initiate the "reform" portion of the New Deal, including:
- Glass-Steagall Act—separated investment from the business of banking
- Securities Exchange Commission (SEC)—helped regulate Wall Street investment practices, making them less dangerous to the overall economy
- Wagner Act—provided worker and union rights to improve relations between employees and employers.
- Social Security Act of 1935—provided pensions as well as unemployment insurance

Other actions focused on insuring bank deposits and adjusting the value of American currency. Most of these regulatory agencies and government policies and programs still exist today.

Labor Regulations

Three major regulations regarding labor that were passed after the Great Depression are:
- The Wagner Act—established that unions were legal, protected members of unions, and required collective bargaining. This act was later amended by the Taft-Hartley Act of 1947 and the Landrum Griffin Act of 1959, which further clarified certain elements.

- Davis-Bacon Act (1931)—provided fair compensation for contractors and subcontractors.
- Walsh-Healey Act (1936)—established a minimum wage, child labor laws, safety standards, and overtime pay.

World War II

<u>Interventionist and Isolationist approaches to involvement</u>
When war broke out in Europe in 1939, President Roosevelt stated that the US would remain neutral. However, his overall approach was considered "interventionist," as he was willing to provide any necessary aid to the Allies short of actually entering the conflict. Thus the US supplied a wide variety of war materials to the Allied nations.

Isolationists believed the US should not provide any aid to the Allies, including supplies. They felt Roosevelt, by assisting the Allies, was leading the US into a war for which it was not prepared. Led by Charles A. Lindbergh, the Isolationists believed any involvement in the European conflict endangered the US by weakening its national defense.

<u>U.S. entry into the war</u>
In 1937, Japan invaded China, prompting the US to halt all exports to Japan. Roosevelt also did not allow Japanese interests to withdraw money held in US banks. In 1941, General Tojo rose to power as the Japanese Premier. Recognizing America's ability to bring a halt to Japan's expansion, he authorized the bombing of Pearl Harbor on December 7, of that year. The US responded by declaring war on Japan. Because of the Tipartite Pact among the Axis Powers, Germany and Italy then declared war on the US, followed by Bulgaria and Hungary.

<u>Surrender of Germany</u>
In 1941, Hitler violated the non-aggression pact he had signed with Stalin in 1939 by invading the USSR. Stalin then joined the Allies. Stalin, Roosevelt and Winston Churchill planned to defeat Germany first, then Japan, bringing the war to an end.

Starting in 1942 through 1943, the Allies drove Axis forces out of Africa. In addition, the Germans were soundly defeated at Stalingrad.

Between July 1943 and May 1945, Allied troops liberated Italy. June 6, 1944, known as D-Day, the Allies invaded France at Normandy. Soviet troops moved on the eastern front at the same time, driving German forces back. April 25, 1945, Berlin was surrounded by Soviet troops. On May 7, Germany surrendered.

<u>Surrender of Japan</u>
War continued with Japan after Germany's surrender. Japanese forces had taken a large portion of Southeast Asia and the Western Pacific, all the way to the Aleutian Islands in Alaska. General Doolittle bombed several Japanese cities while American troops scored a victory at Midway. Additional fighting in the Battle of the Coral Sea further weakened Japan's position. As a final blow, the US dropped two atomic bombs, one on Hiroshima and the other on Nagasaki, Japan. This was the first time atomic bombs had ever been used in warfare, and the devastation was horrific and demoralizing. Japan surrendered on September 2, 1945.

442nd Regimental Combat Team, the Tuskegee Airmen, and the Navajo Code Talkers
The 442nd Regimental Combat Team consisted of Japanese Americans fighting in Europe for the US. The most highly decorated unit per member in US history, they suffered a 93 percent casualty rate during the war. The Tuskegee Airmen were African American aviators, the first black Americans allowed to fly for the military. In spite of not being eligible to become official navy pilots, they flew over 15,000 missions and were highly decorated. The Navajo Code Talkers were native Navajo who used their traditional language to transmit information among Allied forces. Because Navajo is a language and not simply a code, the Axis powers were never able to translate it. Use of Navajo Code Talkers to transmit information was instrumental in the taking of Iwo Jima and other major victories of the war.

Women during World War II
Women served widely in the military during WWII, working in numerous positions, including the Flight Nurses Corps. Women also moved into the workforce while men were overseas, leading to over 19 million women in the US workforce by 1944. Rosie the Riveter stood as a symbol of these women and a means of recruiting others to take needed positions. Women, as well as their families left behind during wartime, also grew Victory Gardens to help provide food.

Atomic bomb
The atomic bomb, developed during WWII, was the most powerful bomb ever invented. A single bomb, carried by a single plane, held enough power to destroy an entire city. This devastating effect was demonstrated with the bombing of Hiroshima and Nagasaki in 1945 in what later became a controversial move, but ended the war. The bombings resulted in as many as 200,000 immediate deaths and many more as time passed after the bombings, mostly due to radiation poisoning.

Whatever the arguments against the use of "The Bomb", the post WWII era saw many countries develop similar weapons to match the newly expanded military power of the US. The impact of those developments and use of nuclear weapons continues to haunt international relations today.

Yalta Conference and the Potsdam Conference

In February 1945, Joseph Stalin, Franklin D. Roosevelt and Winston Churchill met in Yalta to discuss the post-war treatment of Europe, particularly Germany. Though Germany had not yet surrendered, its defeat was imminent. After Germany's official surrender, Clement Attlee, Harry Truman and Joseph Stalin met to formalize those plans. This meeting was called the Potsdam Conference.

Basic provisions of these agreements included:
- Dividing Germany and Berlin into four zones of occupation
- Demilitarization of Germany
- Poland remaining under Soviet control
- Outlawing the Nazi Party
- Trials for Nazi leaders
- Relocation of numerous German citizens
- The USSR joined the United Nations, established in 1945
- Establishment of the United Nations Security Council, consisting of the US, the UK, the USSR, China and France

Post War Japan

General Douglas MacArthur directed the American military occupation of Japan after the country surrendered. The goals the US occupation included removing Japan's military and making the country a democracy. A 1947 constitution removed power from the emperor and gave it to the people, as well as granting voting rights to women. Japan was no longer allowed to declare war, and a group of 25 government officials were tried for war crimes. In 1951, the US finally signed a peace treaty with Japan. This treaty allowed Japan to rearm itself for purposes of self-defense, but stripped the country of the empire it had built overseas.

Alien Registration Act

In 1940, the US passed the Alien Registration Act, which required all aliens older than fourteen to be fingerprinted and registered. They were also required to report changes of address within five days.

Tension between whites and Japanese immigrants in California, which had been building since the beginning of the century, came to a head with the bombing of Pearl Harbor in 1941. Believing that even those Japanese living in the US were likely to be loyal to their native country, the president ordered numerous Japanese to be arrested on suspicion of subversive action isolated in exclusion zones known as War Relocation Camps. Over 120,000 Japanese Americans, two thirds of them citizens of the US, were sent to these camps during the war.

U.S. After World War II

Following WWII, the US became the strongest political power in the world, becoming a major player in world affairs and foreign policies. The US determined to stop the spread of Communism, naming itself the "arsenal of democracy." In addition, America had emerged with a greater sense of itself as a single, integrated nation, with many regional and economic differences diminished. The government worked for greater equality and the growth of communications increased contact among different areas of the country. Both the aftermath of the Great Depression and the necessities of WWII had given the government greater control over various institutions as well as the economy. This also meant the American government took on greater responsibility for the well being of its citizens, both in the domestic arena, such as providing basic needs, and in protecting them from foreign threats. This increased role of providing basic necessities for all Americans has been criticized by some as "the welfare state."

Harry S. Truman

Harry S. Truman took over the presidency from Franklin D. Roosevelt near the end of WW II. He made the final decision to drop atomic bombs on Japan, and he played a major role in the final decisions regarding treatment of post-war Germany. On the domestic front, Truman initiated a 21-point plan known as the Fair Deal. This plan expanded Social Security, provided public housing, and made the Fair Employment Practices Act permanent. Truman helped support Greece and Turkey, under threat from the USSR, supported South

Korea against communist North Korea, and helped with recovery in Western Europe. He also participated in the formation of NATO, the North Atlantic Treaty Organization.

Korean War

The Korean War began in 1950 and ended in 1953. For the first time in history, a world organization—the United Nations—played a military role in a war. North Korea sent Communist troops into South Korea, seeking to bring the entire country under Communist control. The UN sent out a call to member nations, asking them to support South Korea. Truman sent troops, as did many other UN member nations. The war ended three years later with a truce rather than a peace treaty, and Korea remains divided at 38 degrees North Latitude, with Communist rule remaining in the North and a democratic government ruling the South.

Dwight D. Eisenhower

Eisenhower carried out a middle-of-the-road foreign policy and brought about several steps forward in equal rights. He worked to minimize tensions during the Cold War, and negotiated a peace treaty with Russia after the death of Stalin. He enforced desegregation by sending troops to Little Rock, Arkansas when the schools there were desegregated, and also ordered the desegregation of the military. Organizations formed during his administration included the Department of Health, Education and Welfare, and the National Aeronautics and Space Administration (NASA).

John F. Kennedy

Although cut short by his assassination, during his term JFK instituted economic programs that led to a period of continuous expansion in the US unmatched since before WW II. He formed the Alliance for Progress and the Peace Corps, organizations intended to help developing nations. He also oversaw the passage of new civil rights legislation, and drafted plans to attack poverty and its causes, along with support of the arts. Kennedy's presidency ended when he was assassinated by Lee Harvey Oswald in 1963.

Cuban Missile Crisis

The Cuban Missile Crisis occurred in 1962, during John F. Kennedy's presidency. Russian Premier Nikita Khrushchev decided to place nuclear missiles in Cuba to protect the island from invasion by the US. American U-2 planes flying over the island photographed the missile bases as they were being built. Tensions rose, with the US concerned about nuclear missiles so close to its shores, and the USSR concerned about American missiles that had been placed in Turkey. Eventually, the missile sites were removed, and a US naval blockade turned back Soviet ships carrying missiles to Cuba. During negotiations, the US agreed to remove their missiles from Turkey and agreed to sell surplus wheat to the USSR. A telephone hot line between Moscow and Washington was set up to allow instant communication between the two heads of state to prevent similar incidents in the future.

Lyndon B. Johnson

Kennedy's Vice President, Lyndon Johnson, assumed the presidency after Kennedy's assassination. He supported civil rights bills, tax cuts, and other wide-reaching legislation that Kennedy had also supported. Johnson saw America as a "Great Society," and enacted legislation to fight disease and poverty, renew urban areas, support education and environmental conservation. Medicare was instituted under his administration. He continued Kennedy's supported of space exploration, and he is also known, although less positively, for his handling of the Vietnam War.

Civil Rights Movement

In the 1950s, post-war America was experiencing a rapid growth in prosperity. However, African Americans found themselves left behind. Following the lead of Mahatma Gandhi, who lead similar class struggles in India; African Americans began to demand equal rights. Major figures in this struggle included:
- Rosa Parks—often called the "mother of the Civil Rights Movement," her refusal to give up her seat on the bus to a white man served as a seed from which the movement grew.
- Martin Luther King, Jr.—the best-known leader of the movement, King drew on Gandhi's beliefs and encouraged non-violent opposition. He led a march on Washington in 1963, received the Nobel Peace Prize in 1968, and was assassinated in 1968.
- Malcolm X—espousing less peaceful means of change, Malcolm X became a Black Muslim, and supported black nationalism.
- Stokely Carmichael—Carmichael invented the term "Black Power" and served as head of the Student Nonviolent Coordinating Committee. He believed in black pride and black culture, and felt separate political and social institutions should be developed for blacks.
- Adam Clayton Powell—chairman of the Coordinating Committee for Employment, he led rent strikes and other actions, as well as a bus boycott, to increase the hiring of blacks.
- Jesse Jackson—Jackson was selected to head the Chicago Operation Breadbasket in 1966 by Martin Luther King, Jr., and went on to organize boycotts and other actions. He also had an unsuccessful run for President.

Three major events of the Civil Rights Movement are:
- Montgomery Bus Boycott—in 1955, Rosa Parks refused to give her seat on the bus to a white man. As a result, she was tried and convicted of disorderly conduct and of violating local ordinances. A 381-day boycott ensued, protesting segregation on public buses.
- Desegregation of Little Rock—In 1957, after the Supreme Court decision on Brown vs. Board of Education, which declared "separate but equal" unconstitutional, the Arkansas school board voted to desegregate their schools. Even though Arkansas was considered progressive, its governor brought in the National Guard to prevent nine black students from entering Central High School in Little Rock. President Eisenhower responded by federalizing the National Guard and ordering them to stand down.

- Birmingham Campaign—Protestors organized a variety of actions such as sit-ins and an organized march to launch a voting campaign. When the City of Birmingham declared the protests illegal, the protestors, including Martin Luther King, Jr., persisted and were arrested and jailed.

Three major pieces of legislation passed as a result of the Civil Rights movement are:
- Brown vs. Board of Education (1954)—the Supreme Court declared that "separate but equal" accommodations and services were unconstitutional.
- Civil Rights Act of 1964—declared discrimination illegal in employment, education, or public accommodation.
- Voting Rights Act of 1965—ended various activities practiced, mostly in the South, to bar blacks from exercising their voting rights. These included poll taxes and literacy tests.

Minority Rights Expansion

Several major acts have been passed, particularly since WW II, to protect the rights of minorities in America. These include:
- Civil Rights Act—1964
- Voting Rights Act—1965
- Age Discrimination Act—1978
- Americans with Disabilities Act—1990

Other important movements for civil rights included a prisoner's rights movement, movements for immigrant rights, and the women's rights movement. The National Organization for Women (NOW) was established in 1966 and worked to pass the Equal Rights Amendment. The amendment was passed, but not enough states ratified it for it to become part of the Constitution.

Vietnam War

After World War II, the US pledged, as part of its foreign policy, to come to the assistance of any country threatened by Communism. When Vietnam was divided into a Communist North and democratic South, much like Korea before it, the eventual attempts by the North to unify the country under Communist rule led to intervention by the US.
On the home front, the Vietnam War became more and more unpopular politically, with Americans growing increasingly discontent with the inability of the US to achieve the goals it had set for the Asian country. When President Richard Nixon took office in 1969, his escalation of the war led to protests at Kent State in Ohio, during which several students were killed by National Guard troops.

Protests continued, eventually resulting in the end of the compulsory draft in 1973. In that same year, the US departed Vietnam. In 1975, the south surrendered, and Vietnam became a unified country under Communist rule.

US Cold War

The following are US Cold War foreign policy acts and how they affected international relationships, especially between the US and the Soviet Union:

- Marshall Plan—sent aid to war-torn Europe after WW II, largely focusing on preventing the spread of communism.
- Containment—proposed by George F. Kennan, Containment focused on containing the spread of Soviet communism.
- Truman Doctrine—Harry S. Truman stated that the US would provide both economic and military support to any country threatened by Soviet takeover.
- National Security Act—passed in 1947, this act created the Department of Defense, the Central Intelligence Agency, and the National Security Council.

The combination of these acts led to the cold war, with Soviet communists attempting to spread their influence and the US and other countries trying to contain or stop this spread.

NATO, the Warsaw Pact, and the Berlin Wall

NATO, the North Atlantic Treaty Organization, came into being in 1949. It essentially amounted to an agreement among the US and Western European countries that an attack on any one of these countries was to be considered an attack against the entire group.

Under the influence of the Soviet Union, the Eastern European countries of USSR, Bulgaria, East Germany, Poland, Romania, Albania, Poland and Czechoslovakia responded with the Warsaw Pact, which created a similar agreement among those nations.

In 1961, a wall was built to separate Communist East Berlin from democratic West Berlin. A similar, though metaphorical, wall lay between east and west, as well, and was referred to as the Iron Curtain.

Arms Race

After the World War II, major nations, particularly the US and USSR, rushed to develop the atomic bomb, and later the hydrogen bomb, as well as many other highly advanced weapons systems. These countries seemed determined to outpace each other with the development of numerous, deadly weapons. These weapons were expensive and extremely dangerous, and it is possible that the war between US and Soviet interests remained "cold" due to the fear that one side or the other would use these terrifyingly powerful weapons.

Cold War End

In the late 1980s, Mikhail Gorbachev ruled the Soviet Union. He introduced a series of reform programs. Also during this period, the Berlin Wall came down, ending the separation of East and West Germany. The Soviet Union relinquished its power over the various republics in Eastern Europe, and they became independent nations with their own individual governments. With the end of the USSR, the cold war also came to an end.

Technological Advances After WWII

Numerous technological advances after the Second World War led to more effective treatment of diseases, more efficient communication and transportation, and new means of generating power. Advances in medicine increased the lifespan of people in developed countries, and near-instantaneous communication began to make the world a much smaller place.

- Discovery of penicillin (1945)
- Supersonic air travel (1947)
- First commercial airline flight (1948)
- Nuclear power (1951)
- Orbital leading to manned space flight (Sputnik—1957)
- First man on the moon (1969)

Immigration Policy After World War II

Prior to WW II, the US had been limiting immigration for several decades. After WW II, policy shifted slightly to accommodate political refugees from Europe and elsewhere. So many people were displaced by the war that in 1946, The UN formed the International Refugee Organization to deal with the problem. In 1948, the US Congress passed the Displaced Persons Act, which allowed over 400,000 European refugees to enter the US, most of them concentration camp survivors and refugees from Eastern Europe.

In 1952, the President's Escapee Program allowed refugees from Communist Europe to enter the US, as did the Refugee Relief Act, passed in 1953. At the same time, however, the Internal Security Act of 1950 allowed deportation of declared Communists, and Asians were subjected to a quota based on race, rather than country of origin. Later changes included:
- 1962—Migration and Refugee Assistance Act—helped assist refugees in need.
- 1965—Immigration Act—ended quotas based on nation of origin.
- 1986—Immigration Reform and Control Act—prohibited the hiring of illegal immigrants, but also granted amnesty to about three million illegals already in the country.

Richard Nixon

Richard Nixon is best known for illegal activities during his presidency, but other important events marked his tenure as president, including:
- Vietnam War comes to an end
- Improved diplomatic relations between the US and China, and the US and the USSR
- National Environmental Policy Act passed, providing for environmental protection
- Compulsory draft ended
- Supreme Court legalizes abortion in Roe v Wade
- Watergate

The Watergate scandal of 1972 ended Nixon's presidency, when he resigned rather than face impeachment and removal from office.

Gerald Ford

Gerald Ford was appointed to the vice presidency after Nixon's vice president Spiro Agnew resigned under charges of tax evasion. With Nixon's resignation, Ford became president.

Ford's presidency saw negotiations with Russia to limit nuclear arms, as well as struggles to deal with inflation, economic downturn, and energy shortages. Ford's policies sought to reduce governmental control of various businesses and reduce the role of government overall. He also worked to prevent escalation of conflicts in the Middle East.

Jimmy Carter

Jimmy Carter was elected president in 1976. Faced with a budget deficit, high unemployment, and continued inflation, Carter also dealt with numerous matters of international diplomacy including:

- Panama Canal Treaties
- Camp David Accords—negotiations between Anwar el-Sadat, the president of Egypt, and Menachem Begin, the Israeli Prime Minister, leading to a peace treaty between the two nations.
- Strategic Arms Limitation Talks (SALT) and resulting agreements and treaties
- Iran Hostage Crisis—when the Shah of Iran was deposed, an Islamic cleric, the Ayatollah Ruholla Khomeini, came into power. Fifty-three American hostages were taken and held for 444 days in the US Embassy.

Jimmy Carter was awarded the Nobel Peace Prize in 2002.

Ronald Reagan

Ronald Reagan, at 69, became the oldest American president. The two terms of his administration included notable events such as:
- Reaganomics, also known as supply-side or trickle-down economics, involving major tax cuts in the upper income brackets
- Economic Recovery Tax Act of 1981
- First female justice appointed to the Supreme Court, Sandra Day O'Connor
- Massive increase in the national debt—increased from $600 billion to $3 trillion
- Reduction of nuclear weapons via negotiations with Mikhail Gorbachev
- Iran-Contra scandal—cover-up of US involvement in revolutions in El Salvador and Nicaragua
- Deregulation of savings and loan industry
- Loss of the space shuttle Challenger

George Herbert Walker Bush

Reagan's presidency was followed by a term under his former Vice President, George H. W. Bush. His run for president included the famous "thousand points of light" speech, which was instrumental in increasing his standing in the election polls.
During Bush's presidency, numerous major international events took place, including:
- Fall of the Berlin wall and Germany's unification
- Panamanian dictator Manuel Noriega captured and tried on drug and racketeering charges
- Dissolution of the Soviet Union
- Gulf War, or Operation Desert Storm, triggered by Iraq's invasion of Kuwait
- Tiananmen Square Massacre in Beijing, China
- Ruby Ridge
- The arrival of the World Wide Web

William Clinton

William Jefferson Clinton was the second president in US history to be impeached, but he was not convicted, and maintained high approval ratings in spite of the impeachment. Major events during his presidency included:
- Family and Medical Leave Act
- Don't Ask Don't Tell, a compromise position regarding homosexuals serving in the military
- North American Free Trade Agreement, or NAFTA
- Defense of Marriage Act
- Oslo Accords
- Siege at Waco, Texas, involving the Branch Davidians led by David Koresh
- Bombing of the Murrah Federal Building in Oklahoma City, Oklahoma
- Troops sent to Haiti, Bosnia and Somalia to assist with domestic problems in those areas

George W. Bush

Amidst controversy, George W. Bush, son of George Herbert Walker Bush, became president after William Clinton. The election was tightly contested, and though he did not win the popular vote, he won the electoral vote. In the end a Supreme Court ruling was necessary to resolve the issue. His second term was also tightly contested. However, in the election for his second term, Bush won both the popular and the electoral vote. On 9/11/2001, during his first year in office, Bush's presidency was challenged by the first terrorist attack on American soil when al-Qaeda terrorists flew planes into the World Trade Center, destroying it, and into the Pentagon, causing major damage. This event led to major changes in security in the US, especially regarding airline travel. It also led to US troops being deployed in Afghanistan.

Later, Bush initiated war in Iraq with the claim that the country held weapons of mass destruction. On March 20, 2003, the US, along with troops from more than 20 other countries, invaded Iraq. Though no weapons were found, the war continues.

The last months of Bush's administration saw a serious economic meltdown in the US and worldwide. Dramatic increases in oil prices resulted in extreme increases of gasoline prices. This, along with the meltdown of the mortgage industry, created serious and overwhelming economic issues for the Bush administration.

Barack Obama

In 2008, Barack Obama, a Senator from Illinois, became the first African-American US president. His administration has focused on improving the lot of a country suffering from a major recession. His major initiatives have included:
- Economic bailout packages
- Improvements in women's rights
- Moves to broaden gay rights
- Health care reform legislation
- Reinforcement of the war in Afghanistan

History of Georgia

Okefenokee Swamp

The Okefenokee Swamp is the primary swamp in Georgia. It is one of the four largest swamps in the United States. It straddles the Georgia-Florida border. Over the past 6500 years, the swamp has been formed as peat (decaying vegetation) accumulated in a shallow depression on the coastal plain which used to be the mouth of an estuary. High ground around the swamp was likely beach dunes or similar features that have worn down. Most of the swamp is low, jelly-like ground with numerous ponds and waterways through it. Prairies and forests are also found in the swamp. The Okefenokee's water is a dark tea color due to its organic material from rotting vegetation. Native Americans lived in the Okefenokee Swamp as early as 2500 BC, but European exploitation of the swamp only began in the late 1800s. Agriculture of sugar, rice, and cotton was attempted in the 1890s, but after it failed, the swamp was logged for cypress trees. By 1937, the Okefenokee Swamp was named a national wildlife refuge.

Geological Regions

Georgia can be divided into four distinct geologic regions. The northwest corner is the "Valley and Ridge" region, which was formed during the middle Ordovician period when two continental plates collided and formed the Appalachian Mountains. Rippled rock layers in this region alternate between hard and soft layers. The north and northeast part of the state is the "Blue Ridge" region. This area contains the North Georgia Mountains, which are made of rocks formed metamorphically. The region contains many mineral resources, including talc and marble, and once contained gold which has since been mined. The upper half of the state, south of these two regions, is the hilly "Piedmont" region. This region has intermediate elevations that are lower than the northern mountains, but still higher than the coastal plains to the south. The Piedmont terrain was formed by metamorphosis of coastal ocean sediments between 300 and 600 million years ago. The southern portion of the state is the "Coastal Plain" region. This area was more recently coastal ocean sediments, during the Late Cretaceous through Holocene periods 100 million years ago or less. Marine life and dinosaur fossils can be found in the region, and kaolinite minerals are commonly produced there.

Climate and Geography

Georgia's climate is consistent with that of the southeastern United States; summer weather is hot and humid while winter weather is mild. Average winter temperatures do not dip below freezing. The Piedmont and coastal plain regions tend to be much warmer on the whole than the mountain areas. As a result, the growing season in south Georgia is 300 days long, while in north Georgia it is only 185 days. Georgia's economy has historically depended on agricultural products, made possible by its geography and climate. In the 1700s and early 1800s, livestock and subsistence farms were common in the Piedmont and coastal regions. After the cotton gin's invention in 1793, large-scale agricultural efforts focused on cotton. The labor demands of cotton farming led Georgia's economy to depend heavily on slavery, which affected its politics and economic policies.

Cotton is still raised in Georgia, along with other products. Large central forested areas provide lumber, wood pulp, and timber products like turpentine. Chickens, pigs, and cattle are raised throughout the state. Agricultural products also include nuts (pecans and peanuts), peaches, vegetables, and grains like rye.

Waterways

Georgia has more than 71,000 miles of rivers and streams. Most lakes in the state of Georgia are man-made, because the natural landscape does not favor collections of water. The southern part of the state is an exception due to many low areas that accumulate water in and around the Okefenokee Swamp. The Altamaha River watershed includes the Oconee and Ocmulgee Rivers, and is the third largest river on the East Coast of the United States. It flows into the Atlantic Ocean from central and Northeast Georgia. The Ogeechee and Savannah River watersheds flow along the southeast border of the state into the Atlantic. The Satilla and St. Mary's Rivers flow from southeastern Georgia to the Atlantic. The Suwannee and Ochlocknee River Watersheds flow from the southern portion of the state into Florida. The Flint and Chattahoochee Rivers flow southwest from central and Northern Georgia into the Florida Panhandle. The Tallapoosa and Coosa Rivers flow from the northwestern portion of the state into Alabama.

Native Americans

Georgia was first settled by Europeans in 1733, even though white settlers had been in North America for nearly 200 years by then. Europeans displaced Native Americans and brought diseases that Native Americans had no immunity to, so illnesses as simple as a common cold could kill scores of Indians. At first, Georgia settlers negotiated and traded with Native Americans. As the population grew, Indians began to be displaced westward by the colonists, who continually sought more land. Once the United States became independent, it enacted a series of treaties with Indian nations that gradually took away more rights and territory. Georgia passed a law in 1828 that made all Cherokee Indian laws void in 1830. Gold was discovered on Cherokee lands in North Georgia in 1829, which spurred white settlers to remove Native Americans from their lands completely. After a series of legal battles, Georgia lobbied for the creation of the Treaty of New Echota, which was signed in 1835. This Treaty ordered the removal of all Native Americans beyond the Mississippi River within two years.

Early Native Americans living in Georgia were part of the Mississippian culture. These groups built mounds, on which sat temples that overlooked central town areas. These groups had sophisticated religious, trading, and craft traditions. The later Creek Nation is believed to be the descendants of these "Moundbuilders."

The Creek Nation (Muskogee) was a large collection of Native American groups living throughout Georgia before the mid-16th century. These groups were agriculturalists. Contact with white settlers and Cherokee Indians from elsewhere in the southeast forced the Creeks westward, away from the coasts. Creek populations suffered from these land battles and from sickness brought by the whites. Their lands were all taken by 1827.

Cherokee Indians were a large population of Native Americans in the Southeast US. They survived somewhat better than the Creeks because they assimilated white culture and had large numbers of people. They were also affected by illnesses of white settlers. Conflict between the white settlers over land eventually drove Cherokees west along the "Trail of Tears," where thousands of Native Americans died.

Very few Native Americans live in Georgia today. Only 0.3% of the state's population claims a Native American identity. When Cherokees were being rounded up for internment prior to their trip westward during the "Trail of Tears" period, many who escaped joined a group in North Carolina. This particular group had signed a treaty with the US Government in 1819 that had granted them lands separate from the Cherokee Nation (which was taken away during the Treaty of New Echota) and granted them American citizenship. This group, along with the Oconaluftee Indians and escaping Cherokees, formed the Eastern Band of Cherokee Indians. They still live in North Carolina today.

Trail of Tears

The Treaty of New Echota was implemented in 1838. To begin, United States Army troops rounded up all Native American groups in the Eastern states and held them in forts throughout North Carolina, Alabama, Georgia, and Tennessee. Native Americans were treated cruelly during their movement into these internment camps. Eventually, Indian leaders received permission from the US government to remove themselves beyond the Mississippi River. 16 groups of 1,000 Native Americans each went west on the "Trail of Tears." About 3,000 of them traveled west by water, moving up the Tennessee River to the Ohio River, and on to the Arkansas River. The rest traveled west by a number of different land routes. Food was scarce and traveling was difficult. Drought was a constant problem during the removal. 3,000-4,000 people died during the land-route removal. The remaining Cherokees settled along the Illinois River and developed a system of self-governance similar to the US Government. After the Civil War, the Cherokees again lost their land claims and were further marginalized.

American Revolution

Although Georgia sent three delegates to sign the Declaration of Independence in 1776, the colony was not greatly affected by the start of the Revolutionary War. Most of the early fighting took place in the northern colonies or in naval battles. In 1778, Britain captured Savannah and drove the patriot government to Augusta. Fighting at the Battle of Kettle Creek in Wilkes County prevented the entire colony from being occupied. After that battle, Loyalist forces in Georgia were essentially dispersed into the Carolinas. In 1779, American and French forces unsuccessfully laid siege to Savannah, still occupied by the British. Until the end of the Revolutionary War, some loyalists remained along the coast in the only other stronghold than New York. Georgia signed the US Constitution in 1788. The state had eight counties at the time.

Colonial Period

Early settlement began around 1670, when an English settlement was placed near present-day South Carolina. Spanish missions had already been located for 100 years on the Sea Islands of Georgia. Fighting finally drove the Spanish settlers to what is now Florida. In the early 1700s, interest peaked in establishing an English settlement in Georgia.

Georgia was first settled by poor English citizens with permission from King George II in 1733. The colony was a buffer between Florida and South Carolina, and also a place to put English debtors. The citizens were not permitted to govern themselves and were overseen by royally-appointed trustees. Early settlements were organized into townships that were relatively isolated from each other.

Georgia became a royal colony in 1752 when the trustees ceded power over the colony to the King after England stopped providing important subsidies. In 1776, the colony joined 12 others in signing the Declaration of Independence, even though there were many English loyalists in Georgia.

U.S. Constitution

After the United States declared independence from Britain on July 4, 1776, the states worked on a confederation agreement until 1777. The Articles of Confederation were initially signed in 1778 by the first of thirteen states, but it took until 1781 for all states to sign. The Articles of Confederation created a weak national government, and some states objected to the lack of provisions for potential growth. Georgia expected major growth, both in territory and population, and was one of several states that felt the one-state, one-vote philosophy in the Articles was unsatisfying. Georgian signers of the Articles of Confederation were John Walton, Edward Telfair, and Edward Langworthy.

After vigorous debate, the Articles of Confederation were revised into the US Constitution during the summer of 1787. The Constitution set up a strong central government, with distinct responsibilities. Georgia was the fourth state to ratify the US Constitution, signing on January 2, 1788.

The Georgia Constitution of 1777

The Georgia Constitution of 1777 was written to install a constitutional government after large meetings were held throughout the colony in 1776. The constitution was enacted without being ratified by voters, but it set up a large number of procedures that are now considered standard. It put most governmental authority in the state assembly and established a separation of powers. It also ensured the right to freedom of religion, freedom of press, and trial by jury.

The 1777 constitution's description of the governmental setup and the separation of powers was not specific. It also did not provide detailed information about the judicial review system. It did not include a long bill of rights and only spelled out a handful of personal liberties. Slavery and universal suffrage were also not clearly addressed in this constitution. Subsequent constitutions would address all of these issues.

Protestant Religion

During the late 1700s and early 1800s, great religious fervor spread through American Protestant communities. After about 1730, the First Great Awakening significantly altered Protestant philosophies such as Congregational and Presbyterian, and strengthened Baptist and Methodist followings. Methodists believed in personal piety, morality, abolition and evangelism. Baptists believed in conservative philosophies, individual baptism and evangelism. Abolition caused Northern and Southern Methodist churches to split; this split was mended after slavery became illegal. Anti-slavery Methodist teachings may have provided a foothold to the Baptists, whose churches have dominated the southern US ever since.

The Second Great Awakening occurred around 1800, and reached out to people who had not previously been believers. The Baptist and Methodist faiths gained many followers during this time. In the state of Georgia today, these religions are predominant: 39% of residents are Baptist, and 12% of the residents are Methodist.

University of Georgia

The University of Georgia was founded by the Georgia General Assembly in 1785. It was the first university established by a state government. The General Assembly designated 40,000 acres of land to a Senatus Academicus for a college or seminary, and the Senatus began the university in 1799. The college was situated on the banks of the Oconee River. The first classes were held in 1801, and the first class graduated in 1804. The Senatus Academicus was replaced by a Board of Trustees in 1859. The university closed during the Civil War for three years, after which many veterans enrolled. The university added an Agricultural school in 1872 to take advantage of the recent land-grant legislation in the United States government which granted additional land to academic institutions so that they could teach agriculture and mechanics. Females were admitted in 1903 and the first black students were admitted in 1961.

Yazoo Land Fraud

The Yazoo Land Fraud was land speculation that occurred from 1785 to 1803. In 1785, the Combined Society was secretly formed at the same time Bourbon County, GA was founded on the Mississippi River. The Combined Society's purpose was to leverage politicians for land grants, which would then be sold at inflated prices for the Society's gain. Bourbon County was the first parcel of land granted for sale this way. The United States Government pressured Georgia to disband the county in 1788, ending the Combined Society.

In 1789, the South Carolina Yazoo Company, the Virginia Yazoo Company, and the Tennessee Company were formed to buy land from the Georgia legislature. They attempted to buy 20 million acres of land from Georgia for $200,000, but did not succeed because they paid with worthless currency. In 1795, the Georgia Company, the Georgia-Mississippi Company, the Upper Mississippi Company, and the new Tennessee Company bought 40 million acres from Georgia for $500,000. It was later revealed that Georgia officials and legislators held stock in these companies. The sale was nullified in 1796 after public outcry. Money was returned to some buyers, yet others contested the refunds. In 1803 Georgia gave up all lands beyond its current western border, but the Supreme Court ruled in 1810 that sales of these lands had been binding.

Technological Advancements

Eli Whitney patented the cotton gin, which efficiently removed seeds from large quantities of cotton, in 1794. The Georgia climate was well-suited for growing cotton, and large slave-owning plantations could now produce a very lucrative crop. Even though cotton could be seeded easily, slaves were still needed to harvest it by hand. Because of this, the southern economy depended heavily on both slavery and cotton and, by about 1860, cotton provided about 60% of US exports.

After the invention of the spinning jenny in 1770 and the rotary motion steam engine in 1781, large-scale textile factories were built in Britain and the United States. At the same time, railroads were being built throughout the United States from 1785 to 1830. The McCormick reaper was patented in 1830, which allowed even more efficient ways to harvest crops. Cotton and other crops could get to market on the railroads more easily than before, making large-scale agriculture practical even though it was far removed from urban centers. During the American Industrial Revolution from 1810 to 1860, textiles became a large part of the US economy.

Civil War

After the invention of the cotton gin in 1789, slavery was revitalized as the need for field workers increased in Georgia's cotton-producing agricultural lands. The Georgia economy became heavily dependent on the institution of slavery to continue to prosper. At the same time, an economic depression affected the US, increasing the importance of Southern cotton production in the nation's economy. Trade conflicts, such as tariffs designed to promote national commerce and purchase of Northern manufactured products even when international purchases were cheaper, inflamed the agricultural South. States' rights versus federal control became an important issue, and Constitutional interpretation philosophy divided the country into political factions. The rapid growth of Northern populations also threatened to turn areas adhering to Southern philosophies into minority areas. The threat of Northern governments taking away Southerners' personal property (the potential abolition of slavery and the Dred Scott decision) was the last straw that divided the nation.

Georgia seceded from the Union on January 18, 1861. Throughout the war, Georgia's ports were blockaded by Northern fleets, but smugglers brought supplies through the blockade into Georgia's tidal creeks. The war did not come to Georgia until 1863, when the Battle of Chickamauga was fought in northwestern Georgia and southeastern Tennessee. Confederate troops won, but this battle was followed by General Sherman's Atlanta campaign, which captured and burned Atlanta in 1864. Sherman then began the "March to the Sea" campaign, designed to destroy as much of Georgia as possible. Union troops marched from Atlanta to Macon, Milledgeville, and on to Savannah, destroying land and burning homes. After Sherman reached Savannah, he was resupplied by Northern ships and took Savannah in December, 1864. After this, smaller battles and skirmishes occurred in Georgia but the major campaign continued in the Carolinas.

Reconstruction

Reconstruction's overall purpose was to bring Georgia back into the Union, which succeeded by 1872. Other social and economic changes during Reconstruction had lasting effects on the state.

Without slave labor, Southern production was limited. Prisoners in Milledgeville whose labor could be hired cheaply were leased to private companies, like mining operations. In 1908 convict leasing was outlawed, but chain gangs continued to work on public road projects. Convicts still clean roadsides even though they are no longer chained together. In the agricultural regions of Georgia, black citizens and whites who had previously owned small land parcels before the war sharecropped the fields of wealthy landowners until World War II.

Black voters were disenfranchised in the 1890s. The Georgia assembly had no black members from 1907 to 1963. However, public education spread across the state to both black and white citizens. Railroad construction was subsidized to encourage transport of economic products, but the subsidy system was subject to corruption.

Just after the Civil war in 1865, Georgia's economy was depressed due to the social upheaval of Emancipation, physical destruction of agricultural lands, and bad weather. Freed slaves moved to towns where jobs were scarce and disease was common. The Freedmens' Bureau, a new government-formed organization originally designed to aid newly freed slaves in claiming land, helped them develop sharecropping labor agreements with white landowners. These agreements often put former slaves back to work for their previous owners.

From 1866 to 1867, the South was under military occupation. At the same time, laws were passed preventing ex-Confederates from holding office, so officeholders included Freedmen (ex-slaves), carpetbaggers (Northerners who moved South to hold office or help reconstruct the south), and Scalawags (Southern Republicans who had opposed secession). The Ku Klux Klan was formed around this time to promote white supremacy and prevent black education and voting rights.

Unrest from 1868 to 1870 over states' rights and the right of blacks to hold public office led to military rule again in 1869, after which black legislators were readmitted to the state government, making the majority Republican. In 1870, the state was readmitted to the Union. Voting restrictions against ex-Confederates were removed and, by 1872, legislators were largely conservative Democrats.

Populist Movement

The Populist Movement began in about 1892 with the rise of the Populist Party. Poor white farmers in the 1880s and 1890s suffered from low cotton prices, high railroad fees, and debt. They organized the Farmers' Alliance, which demanded that the government print more money to combat economic control by the wealthy. The group campaigned for direct election of congressmen, federal control of the railroads, and banking reform. They also lobbied for the sub-treasury plan, which would allow farmers to borrow against the value of stored crop products while waiting for agricultural prices to improve. Neither the Republican Party nor the Democratic Party supported these ideas, so the Populist Party was formed.

The Populist Party tried to attract Republican blacks and called to end the convict lease system. In the 1896 presidential election, a conservative Republican was elected because the Populist Party split the Democratic vote, after which most Populists returned to the Democratic Party. Black Populists moved back to the Republican Party, having realized that Populist overtures were more about increasing voter numbers rather than addressing black concerns. After 1896, the Populist Party was gone, but its members later successfully disenfranchised Georgia's black voters.

New South

The American South has been called the New South since the Civil War; the term was originally intended to invoke a new reliance on industry instead of slave labor-driven agriculture. Part of the New South philosophy was to encourage railroad construction to promote industry and commerce. Henry Grady, a Georgia journalist, wrote stirringly of the contributions Georgia could make in the New South. As a result of his writing, he was given part ownership of the Atlanta Constitution newspaper. While there, Grady editorialized about his views on temperance laws, veteran healthcare, and library construction. He became heavily involved in Atlanta politics, and leveraged election of pro-industry, pro-urbanization candidates. He campaigned in the North for alliances between Northern and Southern business, which increased investment in Atlanta businesses. Grady's efforts also spurred the founding of the Georgia Institute of Technology and encouraged several cotton expositions in Atlanta that attracted investment and created jobs. Largely as a result of Grady's campaigning, Georgia became an important part of the "New South."

Disenfranchisement

During Reconstruction, the Ku Klux Klan began physically intimidating black voters throughout the South to prevent them from voting. This was outlawed in 1871 with the Force Act of 1870, which authorized the President to use armed forces against people attempting to deny other citizens' Fourteenth Amendment rights. Georgia followed with poll taxes, which were requirements that in order to vote, citizens must have paid taxes or a special poll tax, and must bring the receipt to the polls. Georgia was one southern state that did not use an educational qualification to judge whether a citizen was permitted to vote or not. Other southern states also used grandfather clauses, educational requirements, literacy requirements, or labyrinthine registration procedures to prevent black voters from reaching the polls. Intimidation and economic strategies (like eviction or job loss) were used to prevent blacks from voting in all Southern states until the passage of the Voting Rights Act of 1965.

Jim Crow Laws

Jim Crow laws and customs were developed and applied between 1876 and 1965 to oppress free blacks and prevent them from interacting with whites or reaching equal footing. Each state passed specific laws focusing on black/white interactions. Georgia's major laws were increasingly specific iterations of the following ideas: no intermarriage between races, separate public transportation, separate education, separate prisons and hospitals, and identification of a person with black heritage. Voter registration became increasingly difficult, with the additional requirement that the registrant must correctly answer 10 of 30 very difficult questions designed to confuse the applicant. Laws and customs required alcohol and food sales to be completely separated, and in some states, burials and recreation must be conducted separately. Even though laws provided for "separate but equal" facilities, those for blacks were usually of much lower quality.

Economic Effects of the Boll Weevil and Drought

During World War I, intensive American agriculture efforts to recover maximum wartime profits pushed the land beyond its capacity. Marginal land was cultivated, and this overproduction continued after the war. Surplus production destabilized the economy.

During the 1920s, the United States experienced a period of great prosperity, but the stock market crash of 1929 completely depressed the economy.

At the same time, the boll weevil, a cotton-destroying insect, spread through Georgia beginning in 1915. This drastically reduced cotton production from 5.2 million acres in 1914 to 2.6 million acres by 1923. Insecticides were used, but they were expensive and led to ecological imbalances in insect-predator food webs. Nationwide drought and record heat struck the country from 1933 to 1936, further reducing agricultural production. Georgia's economy between the world wars heavily depended on cotton, and lack of diversification caused the economy to suffer as cotton production declined. The American economy also suffered because agricultural production in the Great Plains essentially ceased when most of the topsoil of this land dried up and blew away in massive dust storms. In the mid to late 1930s, the New Deal attempted to aid the high unemployment rates in Georgia and elsewhere.

World War I

World War I's initial impact on Georgia occurred during the British blockade of European ports that followed the Lusitania sinking and Archduke Ferdinand's assassination. Due to the blockade, Georgia cotton, timber, and naval stores could no longer reach German and Austrian markets, which injured the state's economy and turned citizens against the war. As soon as the United States declared war, Georgia fervently supported the conflict to show that it was committed to American unity and goals. When the draft was instituted, white planters sought to prevent black workers from being drafted. Ultimately the draft was applied statewide and 500,000 men registered from Georgia. Five federal military installations and ten training camps were located in the state. Several of these camps provided specialty training. Many camps were significantly impacted by the 1918 Spanish influenza outbreak. In addition, 130 Georgia soldiers were killed when the HMS Otranto, a troop transport ship, accidentally sank near Scotland in 1918.

After the war, residents of Nashville, Georgia, a town which had lost many soldiers, erected a monument designed by a resident of Americus, Georgia named E.M. Viquesney. He later created more than 150 memorial statues across the nation.

New Deal

Franklin Roosevelt spent a great deal of time in Warm Springs, Georgia for hydrotherapy. While there, he closely examined the relationships between Georgia's social, economic, and educational problems. From 1933 to 1940, New Deal federal aid provided $250 million to Georgia citizens and created programs to address the linkage of these three issues. Roosevelt wanted to enable sharecroppers to become independent, land-owning farmers, and his programs sought to stabilize the agricultural economy with quotas and price adjustments. Unfortunately, these citizens received less economic benefit in reality than was planned. Rural poor citizens received work relief through the Works Progress Administration (WPA), the Civilian Conservation Corps, and the National Youth Administration (NYA). These measures were opposed by more wealthy Georgia citizens, who feared that workers would rather receive higher wages from the government rather than working in the traditional sharecropper structure. Urban housing projects also met resistance from wealthier city dwellers. Eleanor Roosevelt was heavily involved in the Georgia NYA, which encouraged young women and black youths to pursue their educations and provided work at colleges and universities. The egalitarian programs of the New Deal helped black citizens work towards achieving equal employment and equal citizenship.

Eugene Talmadge

Eugene Talmadge was a Georgia native elected four times as Governor. After law school at UGA and public office in Telfair County, he unsuccessfully ran for state legislature twice and then was elected state agriculture commissioner in 1926. He was re-elected twice. Talmadge successfully ran for governor in 1932 and was re-elected in 1934. He was popular with rural farmers, who he attracted with his agricultural knowledge and anti-corporate, evangelical, and white-supremacist philosophies. He condemned the New Deal and warned against its "Communist" tendencies. While governor, Talmadge opposed federal New Deal relief programs. State law prevented him from running a third time in 1936. By the late 1930s, popular opinion in Georgia had turned away from federal relief programs and favored conservative fiscal philosophies. Talmadge again won the 1940 gubernatorial election and spent most of the period dealing with the Cocking affair, in which he leveraged Dean Walter Cocking's firing from the University of Georgia for political reasons. As a result, the University lost accreditation for a year and Georgia public higher education suffered greatly. Talmadge was defeated in 1942, but was re-elected yet again after a change in election law in 1946 with rural support for his Jim Crow platform. He died in December 1946 before taking office.

County-Unit System

The county-unit system was a method of elections used in Georgia from 1917 to 1963, when it was declared unconstitutional. Each county received a set number of votes, and the candidate who won the most votes in that county would win the county unit. 410 county units were divided by population. The eight urban regions would have six unit votes each, the 30 town regions would have four votes apiece, and the 121 rural counties got two votes apiece. This approach skewed the voting power towards rural, low-population areas.

Georgia was dominated by the Democratic Party beginning shortly after Reconstruction, which gave rise to the county-unit system. During the county-unit system, primaries were more important than the final election, and candidates spent a great deal of time seeking county support instead of the popular vote. After the county-unit system was eliminated, candidates needed to spend campaigning time divided by population density. During President Ronald Reagan's term, large numbers of Southerners began to join the Republican Party, which once again created party-based competition during elections. Currently, the balance has changed so much that two-party politics in Georgia are again endangered, only now by the large numbers of Republicans in the state instead of Democrats.

Famous Georgians

Ellis Arnall finished UGA Law School in 1931, was elected to the Georgia House of Representatives in 1932, and became state attorney general in 1938. He became the youngest U.S. governor when he defeated Talmadge for governor in 1942. During his term, Arnall reformed the state constitution, lowered the voting age, paid off state debt, established teachers' retirement and repealed the poll tax. Arnall became an attorney and businessman after Talmadge defeated him in 1946.

Jimmy Carter was elected to the Georgia Senate in 1962 and 1964 after working in the U.S. Navy and on his family's peanut farm. He ran for governor in 1970. He opposed racial segregation and improved state bureaucracies, education, and social programs while governor. He ran for President in 1976. His term occurred during economic stagnation and an energy crisis, but he worked towards social and economic reforms. He also was renowned for conducting significant international diplomacy. Reagan defeated him in 1980, and Carter now works on international relief programs.

Andrew Young was a minister and a civil rights activist elected as a Democratic Congressman in 1972 and re-elected in 1974 and 1976. In 1977 he was appointed Ambassador to the United Nations. He conducted diplomacy with Africa but resigned in 1979 after meeting with Palestinian Liberation Organization leaders. In 1981 Young was elected Atlanta's mayor, and was re-elected in 1985. He ran for governor in 1990 and lost.

Agriculture

Agriculture has always been a key component of Georgia's economy. When the colony was first settled, one of its planned economic activities was exporting agricultural goods to England. Early exports began with corn, and later expanded to include indigo, silk, and wine. Rice also became an important export. After the cotton gin was invented, cotton became a major agricultural commodity.

Today's agriculture in Georgia is more diversified. The state is the number-one producer of young chickens, peanuts, and pecans. It is the second-largest producer of cotton and rye, and is the third-largest producer of peaches and tomatoes. It is the fifth-largest producer of tobacco. Additional crops today include fruits and vegetables, grains, soybeans, and turf grass. Agriculture produces $57 billion of Georgia's $350 billion annual production.

Civil Rights Movement

The civil rights movement in Georgia began with the abolition of slavery. Black communities formed strong schools and churches despite white oppression. They supported national campaigns like Marcus Garvey's Back to Africa movement and the National Association for the Advancement of Colored People (NAACP). During the New Deal, black Georgians had greater access to public assistance and economic opportunity. Racial tension during World War II caused race riots on Georgia's military bases. In 1946, the courts ruled that blacks could vote in Democratic primaries, and black voter registration rose. Officials who would appoint black police and fund black schools were elected in cities. After Eugene Talmadge's 1946 re-election, white supremacy strengthened, and civil rights was associated with Communism through the 1950s. In the early 1960s, the Georgia cities of Albany, Savannah, Atlanta, Brunswick, Macon, and Rome saw significant unrest and protests. Protests in Augusta often generated violence. In rural areas, the civil rights movement stalled because of black poverty and traditional race-based violence. National civil rights legislation in 1964 and 1965 helped, but it did not end the economic problems that contributed to black suppression. Race riots followed in 1965-1970, but large-scale inequality continued through the 1980s, and economic repercussions endure to this day.

Atlanta, the Hartsfield-Jackson International Airport, and the Interstate Highway System

After World War II, Atlanta continued to grow. Companies such as Ford and Bell Aircraft (the early Lockheed Georgia) opened plants in the city. The interstate system increased access. The civil rights movement began to integrate politics and provide increased opportunities to black citizens. Today, Atlanta has become the business hub of the Southeast United States, and is the home base of many corporations including Coca-Cola, Delta Air Lines, CNN, Home Depot, and Georgia-Pacific. It also hosts the Centers for Disease Control.

The Atlanta Municipal Airport, now known as the Hartsfield-Jackson International Airport, was expanded in 1961 and again in 1971. After airline deregulation in 1970, Atlanta became a hub in the new hub-and-spoke system. The airport now provides flights to most continents. It was expanded again in the 1990s, when Atlanta hosted the 1996 Summer Olympic Games.

The Interstate Highway System connects all parts of Georgia with the Southeast, permitting workers to reach their jobs and products to reach their markets. The system was implemented in the 1950s, and was overseen by General Lucius Clay, a Marietta native. One disadvantage of the system is that it has promoted urban sprawl, or uncontrolled spreading, around Atlanta.

Citizen Rights and Responsibilities

The rights of Georgia citizens are spelled out in the state's Bill of Rights. Citizens are free to pursue life, liberty, and property, and these rights are equally protected for all citizens. Religious discrimination is not permitted, and free speech and free press are protected. Citizens may bear arms and have the right to a trial by jury and legal counsel. Penalties in jail and bail amounts must be reasonable, and people may not be tried twice for the same crime unless an appeal is granted or a mistrial is declared. Involuntary servitude is outlawed.

The state government is set up for the benefit of Georgia citizens, and it is their right and responsibility to regulate it and change it. Citizens have the right to vote, so that they may regulate their government and be involved in improving it.

Voting Requirements and Electoral Process

US citizens who are at least 18 years old and reside in Georgia may vote, as long as they have not been convicted of a felony that they have not yet made restitution for. Citizens who are mentally incompetent may not vote. Voter registration can be done by mail at a number of public facilities, but must be completed by 30 days before an election. Elections must be conducted by secret ballot. Elections are conducted annually, and fifteen state-level offices may be elected: governor, lieutenant governor, two senators, secretary of state, attorney general, school superintendent, agriculture commissioner, labor commissioner, insurance commissioner, and five public service commissioners. The Georgia Supreme Court and the Georgia Court of Appeals are also elected. Local offices filled by election also include General Assembly representatives, county, and city officers. Other public authorities may also be elected. Current election procedure uses a touch-screen computer with three backup devices to minimize election problems.

State Constitution

The Georgia State Constitution is intended "to perpetuate the principles of free government, insure justice to all, preserve peace, promote the interest and happiness of the citizen and of the family, and transmit to posterity the enjoyment of liberty" (Constitution, Preamble). To meet these goals, the document lays out regulations governing all aspects of life in Georgia. Previous versions used difficult language that has been eliminated in the current version, which has been revised for clarity and brevity.

The Bill of Rights ensures the basic rights of Georgia citizens. The Voting Article covers who may vote, election rules, and laws governing public officials. The Legislative Branch section describes the composition of the General Assembly and its duties. Constitutional Boards and Commissions describes the setup of state boards and organizations. The Executive Branch section discusses the structure of the Governor's office, the Governor's duties, and the installation and removal procedures for Executive officers. The Judicial Branch Article describes the structure of the courts, rules governing judgeships, and other legal procedures. The Taxation and Finance, Education, and Counties sections discuss specific rules regarding taxation, tax collection, education, and the way the state is divided into counties.

The current Georgia State Constitution is organized into eleven Articles. Each Article is divided into a number of sections. Each paragraph of the section is numbered, and divided into clauses designated with a lower-case letter. Before the first Article, there is a short preamble. In order, the Articles are: Bill of Rights, Voting and Elections, Legislative Branch, Constitutional Boards and Commissions, Executive Branch, Judicial Branch, Taxation and Finance, Education, Counties and Municipal Corporations, Amendments to the Constitution, and Miscellaneous Provisions. At the end, the Constitution includes a table showing the number of amendments proposed, ratified by the General Assembly, and rejected by the General Assembly by year.

Political Parties

Having at least two political parties moderates Georgia's government and provides room for philosophical debate. The first system in the state was the Federalist Party, opposed by the Democratic-Republican Party. By the 1830s, the two parties were the States' Rights Party and the Union Party. These parties merged with the Democratic Party and the Whigs, respectively. The Whig party later collapsed, and Republicans came to Georgia during Reconstruction. Between 1870 and 1960, Georgia was consistently Democratic. After that, Republicans gained a foothold and the two-party system was refreshed. Throughout Georgia's history, third parties have also been key in the outcome of some elections by splitting the vote of one of the main parties, which usually allows the other party to win the election.

In Georgia, a political party is defined by law as a group that received at least 20% of the votes for governor or president in a general election. A political body is a group that can collect 1% of Georgia voters' signatures on a petition or in a statewide election vote. Political bodies may only place candidates on the ballot for local and statewide offices. Third parties must collect signatures equal to 5% of the number of registered voters in order to place a candidate on the ballot for district-office elections.

General Assembly, Governor, and the Lieutenant Governor Qualifications

Georgia General Assembly House members must be 21 years old, have lived in their districts for a year, and in the state for at least two years. Senate members must be 25 years old and meet the same residency requirements. House members serve on committees focused on state business. The committees develop legislation that then passes to the House. The Senate has similar committees. Terms are two years.

The governor must be at least 30 years old, a US Citizen for at least 15 years, and a Georgia resident for at least 6 years. The governor may be elected for two consecutive four-year terms, but must relinquish the position for four years before running again. The governor is the top executive and law enforcement officer, making him the commander in chief of the state's military. He can veto legislation and appoint officials to fill in gaps until the next election. He also oversees the state budget and can award discretionary money to specific projects.

The lieutenant governor must meet the same qualifications as the governor. He may be re-elected an unlimited number of times. This office is voted separately from the governor. The lieutenant governor fills the governor's office until the next general election if the governor cannot hold office and presides over the state senate. Informal duties of this office are to appoint members to statewide committees.

General Assembly

The Georgia General Assembly is divided into two chambers, the House of Representatives (180 members; lower house) and the Senate (56 members; upper house). Each chamber is divided into committees whose party composition is the same as that of the chamber. These committees discuss and debate issues that affect the state. The leader of the House of Representatives is the Speaker of the House, who is a member of the majority political party and who is elected by the entire chamber. This person schedules debates, votes, and can assign representatives to committees. The majority and minority parties are also presided over by the majority and minority leader, whose functions are to advance their parties' interests. If a bill is approved by the House, it passes to the Senate. The Senate is also divided into committees which debate and introduce legislation. The lieutenant governor presides over the Senate instead of a Speaker. The president pro tempore of the Senate is the leader of the majority party.

Duties of the Georgia Assembly include introducing new legislation, amending the Georgia State Constitution, passing the state budget every year, and re-drawing legislative districts every decade.

Issues raised in the Georgia House of Representatives begin when a legislator drafts a bill or resolution. He usually relies on the Office of Legal Counsel to write the actual text to make sure it is in the correct format. The bill summary, or title, is read aloud on the floor of the house on three separate days. The bill is assigned to a committee for consideration. Bills that are favorably considered by their committees are forwarded to consideration by the entire House. Debates and questions follow, amendments may be suggested, and the bill is voted on. If it passes the House, it moves on to the Senate. The same process occurs, and the bill is sent back and forth between House and Senate until it is either rejected or approved upon by both bodies. If approved, the bill is then sent on to the governor for consideration. He may sign the bill within 40 days or he may veto it. His veto can be overridden by a two-thirds majority of the Senate.

County Governments

Currently, there are 159 counties in Georgia. The large number of counties reflects Georgia's rural history; nearly each town was a county seat, which gave rural residents a cultural, judicial, and political center and also enhanced their representation in state government.

Counties' duties are numerous. They issue license plates and taxes, hold court, register voters, maintain roads, administer public assistance, probate wills, maintain police and fire forces, oversee garbage collection and hospitals, manage parks and recreation, govern sewage and water management, build libraries, and preserve building codes. These numerous roles provide all of Georgia's citizens with services similar to those available in cities, even if they live in rural areas.

City Governments

In Georgia, cities and towns operate under a charter of municipal incorporation approved by the state assembly, which controls their existence and boundaries. The charter describes the basic governmental structure of the city.

The city government oversees anything pertaining to public life. This includes protecting the citizens in emergencies with fire and police responders, protecting the environment and overseeing solid and sewer sanitation, levying taxes, spending money on public works, managing public transportation and roads, and planning laws for city growth and zoning.

City governments in Georgia are one of three types: the strong mayor-council, the weak mayor-council, or the council-manager. In the strong mayor-council form, the mayor represents the executive branch and the council represents the legislative branch. The mayor oversees the running of the government and the council adopts legislation and ordinances that dictate government policies. The weak mayor-council form shares the duties between the mayor and the city council. The mayor is the primary executive body, but his or her duties may also be primarily ceremonial. In the council-manager format, the city council decides policy and hires a manager to carry them out.

State Programs

Georgia state programs fall mainly into executive, legislative, and judicial categories. Executive programs include the Department of Agriculture; the Department of Labor; Insurance and Fire Safety; Public Services; and the offices of Executive members which includes the governor, lieutenant governor, attorney general, secretary of state, and the state school superintendent. These programs are all designed to protect and improve the lives of Georgia citizens. Legislative programs include the General Assembly, voting, lawmaking, and districting. These programs are intended to permit Georgia citizens to participate in their government. Judicial programs include all the courts of the state, which are in place to protect the liberties of citizens and to address any wrongdoing.

Court System

The Georgia court system has limited, general, and appellate courts. Limited-jurisdiction courts include magistrate courts, probate courts, county courts, and juvenile courts. These courts oversee smaller legal issues, such as small civil suits, violation of county ordinances, misdemeanors, traffic violations, juvenile violations and issuing search warrants. General-jurisdiction courts are the superior courts of the state, and they oversee any felony and any civil or criminal case. Appellate-jurisdiction courts are the Court of Appeals and the Supreme Court. These courts rule on cases generated in the other two levels of the judicial system.

Except for juvenile courts, judges of limited-jurisdiction courts are elected every four years in general or partisan elections by the geographic unit over which they would preside. Juvenile court judges are appointed by superior court judges in four-year terms. Part-time judges may continue to work as lawyers separately from their judicial work. General-jurisdiction, or superior court judges, are also elected for four-year terms by the public. Appellate court judges are elected for six-year terms by the public.

Juvenile and Adult Justice Systems

The juvenile justice system of Georgia is applied to delinquent children under the age of 17 and deprived children under 18. In situations concerning capital felonies, custody, and parental rights, the juvenile justice system works with the superior courts. Juvenile courts oversee issues of traffic violations as well as violent felonies such as murder, rape, and armed robbery. Trials are not conducted in front of a jury, and issues go directly to the Court of Appeals or the Supreme Court if there is a problem. Designated detention centers are used for juvenile offenders, and rehabilitation is an important goal.

The adult justice system applies to everyone over the age of 17. Trials are typically conducted in front of a jury unless the issue is addressed in magistrate court. Probate and magistrate issues may be addressed in Superior Court before they are sent to the Court of Appeals or Supreme Court. Sentencing tends to be harsher than in the juvenile system.

Practice Test

Practice Questions

1. Where was the first great human civilization located?
    a. Egypt
    b. Greece
    c. Mesopotamia
    d. Samaria

2. Which of the following was not an ancient Egyptian ruler?
    a. Anubis
    b. Hatshepsut
    c. Ramses' II
    d. Tutankhamen

3. How did the Crusader army that went on the First Crusade differ from the Crusader armies that Pope Urban II envisioned?
    a. There was no difference. The people of Europe were accustomed to obeying clerical direction and eagerly joined the cause creating an army that was primarily made up of faithful Christians from all social classes led by a select group of knights who were responsible for leading and training their armies.
    b. There was no difference. The people of Europe obeyed clerical direction and stayed home to pray for the success of an army composed entirely of knights and professional other military personnel.
    c. Pope Urban II had envisioned an army of skilled knights and professional soldiers; instead, men and women from all classes joined together to retake the Holy Land.
    d. Pope Urban II had envisioned an army composed of faithful Christians of from all social classes led by a group of select knights; instead the army was primarily made up of knights and other professional military personnel.

4. Which western European monastic order developed an early form of banking that helped make pilgrimages to the Holy Land safer for the pilgrims?
    a. The Knights Templar
    b. The Knights Hospitaller
    c. The Knights of Malta
    d. The Barbary Corsairs

5. Which early feminist work was written by Mary Wollstonecraft?
    a. A Vindication of the Rights of Woman
    b. The Declaration of Sentiments
    c. Frankenstein
    d. The Awakening

6. What is the historical significance of the Dome on the Rock's site to Jews?
    a. It is the traditional site of Jesus Christ's crucifixion and resurrection
    b. It is located on Temple Mount, where the Second Temple previously stood and the traditional site of Solomon's Temple
    c. It is the traditional site of Mohammed's ascent into heaven
    d. It is the site of the founding of the Islamic religion.

7. How did the Nile shape the Ancient Egyptian Empire?
    a. It provided a nonnavigable boundary for the Egyptian Empire.
    b. It eroded land, creating natural harbors for Egyptian fishermen.
    c. It routinely flooded, eroding the limited desert farmland.
    d. It routinely flooded, leaving behind fertile silt that helped make large scale agriculture possible.

8. In which country does a large part of the native, traditionally nomadic people currently live in large tents known as yurts or gers?
    a. Indonesia
    b. Mongolia
    c. Thailand
    d. India

9. Which of the following was not a tax levied on the American colonies by the British government in the 1760's and 70's?
    a. The Sugar Act of 1764
    b. The Stamp Act of 1765
    c. The Lead Act of 1772
    d. The Tea Act of 1773

10. To whom was the Declaration of Independence addressed and why?
    a. To the British Parliament, because the colonists were opposed to being ruled by a king who had only inherited his throne and only considered the popularly elected Parliament to hold any authority over them
    b. To the King of England because the colonists were upset that Parliament was passing laws for them even though they did not have the right to elect members of Parliament to represent their interests.
    c. To the Governors of the rebelling colonies so that they would know that they had 30 days to either announce their support of the Revolution or to return to England.
    d. To the colonial people as a whole. The Declaration of Independence was intended to outline the wrongs that had been inflicted on them by the British military and inspire them to rise up in protest.

11. How did the ruling in Marbury v. Madison alter the Supreme Court's power in the federal government?

    a. It lessened it. The Supreme Court was concerned about the possibility of judges overturning laws enacted by voters through referendums and took away that power.
    b. It increased it. The decision in Marbury v. Madison gave the Supreme Court it's now traditional right to overturn legislation.
    c. It increased it. The decision in Marbury v. Madison strengthened the Supreme Court's Constitutional right to overturn legislation.
    d. There was no change. Marbury v. Madison was a case involving a president who was unwilling to obey laws enacted by his predecessor; there was nothing about the case or decision that would have more than a cursory connection to federal powers of government

12. Which President of the United States changed the date of Thanksgiving from the last Thursday of November to the fourth Thursday of November?

    a. George Washington
    b. Andrew Jackson
    c. Abraham Lincoln
    d. Franklin D. Roosevelt

13. Which of the following is an example of historiography?

    a. An explanation of past treatments of an historical event.
    b. A geographer using physical geography to explain historical events.
    c. A historical treatise on a single aspect of a larger historical event.
    d. Historiography is not a valid historical term

14. Which of the following questions would most likely be asked by a historian concerned with the philosophy of history?

    a. What issues shaped the writing of Plato's Republic?
    b. Should history be measured by changes in individual lives or by larger political trends?
    c. Why were the religions of Shinto and Buddhism able to merge in Japan?
    d. Should historians study modern primitive cultures as a means of learning about past civilizations?

15. You are researching the Battle of the Bulge's Malmedy Massacre. Four potential sources offer conflicting accounts of one aspect of the event. Based on the principles of historical research, which source is most likely to be accurate?

    a. Wikipedia
    b. A newspaper article written by a reporter who interviewed several surviving soldiers over the weeks following the massacre.
    c. The account of a wounded survivor written immediately following the massacre.
    d. One of your teaching colleague's lecture notes.

16. Which of the following is considered to be the largest cause of death among Native Americans following the arrival of European colonists in North America?
    a. Wounds from wars with the European settlers
    b. Wounds from wars with the other Native American tribes
    c. European diseases
    d. Exposure during the wintry, forced marches on which the European settlers forced them

17. What is the historical significance of the Dome on the Rock's site to Muslims?
    a. It is the traditional site of Jesus Christ's crucifixion and resurrection
    b. It is located on Temple Mount, where the Second Temple previously stood and the traditional site of Solomon's Temple
    c. It is the traditional site of Mohammed's ascent into heaven
    d. It is the site of the founding of the Islamic religion.

18. What method did Johannes Gutenberg use to create printing plates for his printing press?
    a. Woodcuts – he had a team of apprentices carve each page out of wood plates.
    b. Metal etchings – the letters were etched into specially treated metal plates which were then placed in special acid baths to create printing plates.
    c. Moveable clay type – Gutenberg carved moveable type out of clay and would press the letters into hot wax tablets to create printing plates.
    d. Moveable type – Gutenberg cast metal type through the use of molds in order to achieve the individual letters which were then loaded into composing sticks, which were then used to form printing plates.

19. Which group(s) of people were originally responsible for selecting the members of the U.S. Senate?
    a. State legislatures
    b. State governors
    c. State electors
    d. State residents, subject to voting eligibility

20. The Erie Canal is 363 miles long and connects which body of water to Lake Erie?
    a. The Mississippi River
    b. The Hudson River
    c. The Susquehanna River
    d. The Lehigh River

21. The telephone was a solution to which of the following problems with the telegraph?
    a. Telegraph lines were thick and difficult to maintain.
    b. Telegraph messages could only be received by people who had specialized equipment.
    c. Telegraphs could only relay one message at a time.
    d. Telegraphs frequently broke down if subject to extended use.

22. Why did each Incan ruler have to earn his own fortune?
    a. A tradition that all the wealth an Incan king accumulated during his reign would be used to house and care for the king's mummified remains.
    b. A tradition that all of a deceased king's wealth would be added to the main Incan temple's treasury.
    c. A tradition that all of a deceased king's wealth would be used to create a large public work in the king's memory.
    d. A belief that the new king needed to prove his worth through conquest and adding to the royal treasury.

23. How would this picture be most appropriately used?
    a. As an example of a Suffragist picket sign.
    b. As an example of American response to Versailles Treaty.
    c. As an example of early American use of Biblical allusions.
    d. As an example of an early American response to the German Nazi movement.

Records Administration.
http://teachpol.tcnj.edu/amer_pol
_hist/thumbnail297.html

24 .What was the ancient Agora of Athens?
    a. It was the main temple to Athena, where scholars would go to give lectures and pray for wisdom.
    b. It was the Athenian ruling body.
    c. It was the city of Athens's main source of drinking water and a place where Athenian women traditionally gathered.
    d. It was the name of the primary marketplace and also an important gathering center for Athenians.

25. Who was Genghis Khan?
    a. The founder of the Mongol Empire
    b. The leader of the Hunnic Empire in the 5th Century who led his people to attack into Western Europe.
    c. The leader of the 19th Century Taiping Rebellion
    d. None of the above

26. Which of the following is not necessarily an example of an educator introducing his own bias into the educational process?
    a. A teacher only using materials and sources that he knows are reputable and declining to use unverified material in his lessons.
    b. A textbook author choosing to only use sources that place his favorite U.S. president in a good light and his least favorite U.S. president in a bad light.
    c. A teacher only using primary sources that he agrees with and ridiculing a student who provides a verifiable primary source that offers a conflicting opinion.
    d. All of the above are examples of bias

27. Which of the following words can be defined as "a list events organized in order of their occurrence?"
    a. Anachronism
    b. Anno Domini
    c. Chroma
    d. Chronology

28. Who was Lewis and Clark's guide?
    a. Pocahontas
    b. Sacagawea
    c. Squanto
    d. Wauwatosa

29. What was the standard government economic principle in the late nineteenth and early twentieth centuries?
    a. Laissez faire
    b. Social Darwinism
    c. Keynesian Economics
    d. Monetarism

30. What was the purpose of Lyndon Johnson's Great Society?
    a. To eliminate poverty and racial injustice in America
    b. To erase the last vestiges of the Great Depression from the American economic landscape.
    c. To encourage economic prosperity through trickledown economics.
    d. To increase educational standards in the United States.

31. What were Woodrow Wilson's Fourteen Points?
    a. A list of reasons why women should not be given the right to vote.
    b. A list of conditions to which France and Great Britain had to agree before the United States would enter World War I.
    c. His plan for the rehabilitation of Germany after World War I
    d. His plan for stimulating the economy and turning the United States into a major economic power.

32. Which of the following American cities was not founded by people fleeing religious persecution?
    a. Plymouth, Massachusetts
    b. Jamestown, Virginia
    c. Boston, Massachusetts
    d. Providence, Rhode Island

33. Which of the following is an example of providing a connection between history and economics?
    a. Using maps showing post-World War II migration patterns.
    b. Using charts and maps to illustrate the growth of U.S. cities.
    c. Discussing the effects of weather on world history.
    d. Discussing the role of food shortages and inflation in the Russian Revolution.

34. Which economic crisis led to the creation of the SEC?
    a. The Panic of 1907
    b. The Post World War I Recession
    c. The Great Depression
    d. The Recession of 1953

35. What was the purpose of the Mayflower Compact?
   a. To create and enact a series of laws for the Pilgrims.
   b. To create a temporary government for the Pilgrims.
   c. To memorialize the Pilgrims' promises to raise their children according to their religious ideals.
   d. To memorialize the laws under which the Pilgrims had previously been living

36. What was Manifest Destiny?
   a. The idea that the United States was intended by God to expand to fill North America.
   b. The idea that England was intended by God to expand its empire to fill the world.
   c. The idea that England was intended by God to colonize the non-European world.
   d. The idea that the United States was intended by God to spread democracy throughout the world.

37. What was the purpose of the Marshall Plan?
   a. To rebuild Europe after World War I and strengthen the United States' Western allies.
   b. To rebuild Europe after World War II and prevent the spread of Communism in post-war Europe.
   c. To create jobs for U.S. servicemen following World War II.
   d. To build hospitals for wounded war veterans following World War I.

38. Most of the earliest civilizations flourished in or near what sort of geographic feature?
   a. Mountains
   b. Valleys
   c. Oceans
   d. Rivers

39. Which of the following is a true statement concerning the Magna Carta?
   a. It's main purpose was to prevent the Church from increasing its holdings.
   b. It created a system of majority rule in England.
   c. It was meant to protect the rights and property of the few powerful families that topped the feudal system.
   d. It was concerned with the rights of all Britons and frequently mentions the common people.

40. Which statement is an accurate reflection of Mayan urban life?
   a. The Mayas were a sophisticated urbanized culture, whose people predominately lived in large cities.
   b. The Mayas lived in urban communities, supported by a small number of highly productive farms.
   c. Mayan cities were primarily used as religious centers.
   d. Mayan cities were primarily used as government centers.

41. What were Martin Luther's 95 theses?
   a. His charter for the Lutheran Church
   b. Criticisms of practices in the Catholic Church
   c. A document explaining his differences with other Protestant churches
   d. Reasons why the Bible should be translated into popular languages.

42. Which U.S. Founding Father is credited with founding the Federalist Party?
    a. John Adams
    b. Thomas Jefferson
    c. Alexander Hamilton
    d. George Washington

43. Who were the Shoguns?
    a. Chinese military leaders
    b. Japanese military leaders
    c. Chinese religious leaders
    d. Japanese religious leaders

44. Which of the following is a true statement concerning the Iroquois Confederacy?
    a. It was a Confederacy of French fur trappers and settlers and members of the Iroquois tribes during the French and Indian War.
    b. It was a group of seven Native American tribes who joined together to protect themselves against European incursions into their territories.
    c. Its members were also known as the Five Civilized Tribes.
    d. It made decisions through a democratic process.

45. Which of the following was one of reasons that James Oglethorpe wished to found the colony of Georgia?
    a. To create an escape-proof penal colony in North America.
    b. To create a refuge for England's "worthy poor."
    c. To increase the Virginia Company's profitability
    d. To build a new port city to aid in the existing colonists' plans for westward expansion.

46. Which of the following is not a true statement concerning the beginnings of slavery in the Virginia colony?
    a. Slavery was established quickly as a means of securing a cheap source of labor.
    b. Initially slaves could become free through converting to Christianity.
    c. The number of slaves in Virginia increased as tobacco planters required a steady supply of labor.
    d. Early Virginian slaves included both Africans and Native Americans.

47. Why were the "Five Civilized Tribes" given that name?
    a. They had advanced military systems.
    b. In recognition of the assistance they gave early European settlers.
    c. They had advanced social and government systems.
    d. They had formed a complex Confederacy dedicated to preserving peace amongst themselves.

48. Who famously crossed the Rubicon in 49 BC?
    a. Julius Caesar
    b. Cleopatra
    c. Mark Antony
    d. Marcus Brutus

49. What was the basis of Edward Jenner's original smallpox vaccine?
    a. Liquid from chickenpox sores
    b. Liquid from cowpox sores
    c. Liquid from smallpox sores
    d. Liquid from acne sores

50. Which Japanese city was the first to be attacked with an atomic bomb?
    a. Hiroshima
    b. Nagasaki
    c. Nagoya
    d. Tokyo

51. Which of the following peoples did not practice a form of feudalism?
    a. The Norsemen (Vikings)
    b. The Germans
    c. The Persians
    d. The Byzantines

Use the following passage to answer questions 52-54:

> The United States' Constitution is the longest-lived written constitution in world history and has served as the model for the constitutions of other nations. Several factors contribute to its survival into the twenty-first century, the most important being the Constitution's simplicity and the built-in permission to amend it as necessary.
>
> Simplicity gives the Constitution flexibility. In it, basic rules do not change but within these rules, laws and practices can and are modified to meet the needs of the people and the state. If the Constitution had specific rules and laws concerning dynamic forces such as the economy, it would have quickly become outmoded or obsolete as the United States came to face challenges and situations that the original framers could not have predicted. The Constitution's framers realized that they could not anticipate the future and so created a document that provided a basic framework of government that could be amended without being cast aside as new situations and needs arose. This ability to amend the Constitution aided the pro-Constitution Federalists in the fight to ratify it as they gained support with the promise of the Bill of Rights which soothed early concerns regarding the rights of man.

52. Assuming that the above passage was from a student's essay, which of the following questions would it best answer?
    a. How is the U.S. Constitution a simple document?
    b. Why was the United States' Constitution used as a model for other countries' constitutions?
    c. Which attributes have contributed to the U.S. Constitution's longevity?
    d. What was the Federalist Party's earliest public action?

53. Which of the following is the best explanation of how the information in the above passage could be used in a class focused on a subject other than History?
    a. To describe the formation of the U.S. Constitution in a government class.
    b. To explain the basis of U.S. law in a government class.
    c. To explain why the U.S. Constitution can be amended in a current events class
    d. To describe attributes of the U.S. Constitution in a government class.

54. How could the information in the above passage be used to form a connection between history and modern government?
    a. To explain how Enlightenment ideas shaped American legal theory.
    b. To explain why the Constitution's framers chose to create a basic framework for government rather than create a strict, unchangeable model.
    c. To explain how the American two-party political system began.
    d. To explain why it was necessary to have a written Constitution.

55. Which of the following was a contemporary argument against The Bill of Rights?
    a. The concern that it didn't apply to the states.
    b. The belief that a bill of rights would infringe upon states' rights.
    c. The concern that specifically stating one right would create an argument against an unstated right.
    d. The belief that the Bill of Rights would be too great a check on government's ability to function.

56. What were the Federalist Papers meant to accomplish?
    a. To encourage people to join the Federalist Party
    b. To explain the necessity of the federalist system
    c. To assist in the ratification of the Constitution
    d. To expose a series of scandals relating to the Federalist Party

57. What was Franklin D. Roosevelt's "court packing" plan?
    a. A plan to influence court outcomes by packing the observation gallery with his own supporters.
    b. A plan to prevent cases from coming to trial by filing a large number of other cases in order to create judicial gridlock.
    c. A plan to keep Roosevelt surrounded by his own supporters to give him a greater impression of popularity.
    d. A plan to appoint a second justice for every federal justice over the age of seventy.

58. How did the invention of the cotton gin change the cotton industry in the United States?
    a. It decreased the amount of labor needed to grow cotton, thereby decreasing the demand for slaves.
    b. It had no overall effect on the cotton industry.
    c. It made Southern cotton plantations dependant on Northern textile factories who could use the gins to efficiently clean cotton.
    d. It turned cotton into a viable cash crop resulting in cotton becoming a major Southern export.

59. What was the purpose of the Sherman Anti-Trust Act?
    a. To prevent unions from striking
    b. To prevent restraints on free trade
    c. To encourage international trade
    d. To prevent corporate tax evasion

60. What did the landmark Supreme Court case, *Brown v. The Board of Education of Topeka* decide?
    a. That school busing was inherently Constitutional.
    b. That the doctrine of separate but equal was Unconstitutional.
    c. That racially separate educational facilities deprive people of equal protection under the laws.
    d. That Plessy v. Ferguson was appropriately decided.

61. Which of the following did not occur during or because of the French Revolution?
    a. The Reign of Terror
    b. Economic crisis
    c. The ending of feudal practices and slavery in France
    d. The calling together of the Estates General

62. Before 1854, which of the following countries had regular trading relations with Japan?
    a. The Netherlands
    b. Great Britain
    c. France
    d. Italy

63. Which of the following was a power granted to the U.S. Congress under the Articles of Confederation?
    a. The power to collect taxes
    b. The power to enter into treaties with foreign governments
    c. The power to enforce laws
    d. The power to regulate interstate commerce

64. According to Plato's *Republic*, which sort of person would make the best head of state?
    a. A philosopher
    b. A great general
    c. An elderly farmer
    d. A young noble, trained for rule from birth

65. Which of the following was not an effect of the Neolithic agricultural revolution?
    a. The establishment of social classes
    b. The building of permanent settlements
    c. An overall increase in leisure time
    d. All of the above were effects of the Neolithic agricultural revolution

66. Which of the following U.S. Constitutional Amendments lowered the voting age to eighteen?
    a. The 24th
    b. The 25th
    c. The 26th
    d. The 27th

67. Which of the following is an effect that mountains can have on a society?
    a. Acting as a source of food
    b. Protecting the society from invasion
    c. Providing a means of cultural diffusion
    d. Providing a source of transportation

68. Which statement is the best summary of the Monroe Doctrine?
    a. That European powers were not to interfere with the affairs of North America
    b. That no European power could forbid the United States from trading with another sovereign state
    c. That European powers were to not to interfere with affairs in the Western Hemisphere and that the United States would stay out of affairs in Europe.
    d. None of the Above

69. Who was the first President of South Africa to be elected in a fully representative South African election?
    a. Mahatma Gandhi
    b. Thabo Mbeki
    c. Kgalema Motlanthe
    d. None of the above

70. Which of the following events was a proximate cause of World War I?
    a. The Japanese bombing of Pearl Harbor
    b. The assassination of the Austrian-Hungarian Empire's Archduke Ferdinand
    c. The sinking of the RMS Lusitania
    d. The British interception of the Zimmerman telegram

71. Who was Boris Yeltsin?
    a. A Russian politician credited with breaking up the USSR
    b. A Russian politician who was instrumental in the Russian Revolution
    c. A Ukrainian politician who encouraged his country to break away from the Eastern bloc countries
    d. A Scandinavian politician who successfully prevented his country from joining the Warsaw Pact

72. Which of the following best describes The Truman Doctrine?
    a. The United States has the sole authority to assist other democracies located in North and South America.
    b. The United States must not interfere with the internal struggles of countries outside the Western Hemisphere.
    c. The United States must support free peoples who are resisting attempted subjugation by armed minorities or by outside pressures.
    d. None of the above

73. In 1955 the Soviet Union formed the Warsaw Treaty Organization to counterbalance which of the following?
    a. NAFTA
    b. NATO
    c. The U.N. Security Counsel
    d. The Four Power Pact

74. Which of the following was an advantage that the South held over the North at the beginning of the Civil War?
    a. Greater industry and capability to produce war materials
    b. Larger population/more available manpower
    c. Better railroad system
    d. Better military commanders

75. Which of the following was not one of the ways that the Mormon migration was unique among the American pioneers?
    a. They transported an entire culture across the American West.
    b. They traveled as highly organized companies.
    c. They improved the trail, built ferries and, planted crops as a means of assisting those who would follow them
    d. All of the above

76. Which of the following was a long term effect of the New Deal?
    a. The end of the Great Depression
    b. An increase in the role the federal government played in the U.S. economy.
    c. Decreased price supports for U.S. farmers
    d. All of the above

77. Who was César Chávez?
    a. The leader of a movement to improve working conditions for migrant laborers.
    b. A civil rights leader who worked to improve inner city conditions.
    c. A civil rights leader who dedicated his life to immigration reform
    d. None of the above

78. Which of the following is not a result of the Civil Rights Movement's work in the 1950s and 60s?
    a. The government enacted legislation prohibiting racial discrimination in employment.
    b. Disenfranchisement of African Americans was declared illegal.
    c. Court rulings that segregation in schools violated the Constitution led to a near instantaneous desegregation of public educational facilities.
    d. The government enacted legislation prohibiting racial discrimination in the housing market.

79. Which of the following was an effect of industrialization in the United States?
    a. Large growth in city populations
    b. A general shift from self-employment to being employed by others
    c. Increased economic/employment opportunities for women
    d. All of the above

80. Which of the following were causes of The Dust Bowl?
   I. Wind erosion
   II. Too many cultivated fields being left fallow at once
   III. Severe droughts
      a. I, II, & III
      b. I & II
      c. I & III
      d. II & III

81. Enlightenment principles signaled a departure from which of the following types of government rule?
      a. Monarchy
      b. Democracy
      c. Anarchy
      d. Republicanism

82. What was the first well-known American school of painting?
      a. The Boston Revolutionaries
      b. The Savannah Art School
      c. The New York Artists' Guild
      d. The Hudson River School

83. What does the Communist Manifesto claim makes up all of history?
      a. Battles between political ideas
      b. Class struggles
      c. Battles to control the means of production
      d. None of the above

84. In a market economy, what is the theoretical basis for the price of an individual good?
      a. Central Control
      b. Supply and Demand
      c. Cost Gouging
      d. Income and Industry

85. Which of the following is a way that the Internet affected world wide economies?
      a. It made near instantaneous communication possible.
      b. It caused an overall increase in the cost of transactions.
      c. It increased consumer access to goods.
      d. It increased the barriers to entry in retail situations.

86. Which of the following was a method that the government in Nazi Germany used gain control of German children?
      a. Mandating membership in government sponsored youth organizations
      b. Including propaganda in textbooks
      c. Mandating activities scheduled to conflict with church services and interfere with family life
      d. All of the above

87. What was the purpose of John Locke's Two Treatises on Government?
    a. To support the results of the Glorious Revolution
    b. To provide support for the American Revolution
    c. To provide support for the French Revolution
    d. To provide support for the Irish Revolution

Use the following statistical table to answer Question 88

Median U.S. income by amount of schooling, in dollars
Source: U.S. Census Bureau, Current Population Survey, Annual Social and
Economic Supplements.

Year	9-12th grade, no diploma	High School graduate	Some College, no degree	Associates Degree	Bachelors Degree or higher
2007	24,492	40,456	50,419	60,132	84,508
2002	23,267	35,646	45,333	51,058	73,600
1997	19,851	33,779	40,015	45,258	63,292

88. Which of the following could you infer from the data presented above?
    a. Persons without a high school diploma receive smaller monetary increases in their income than persons with a high school diploma.
    b. Increased education increases a person's earning potential
    c. Income generally increases over time.
    d. All of the above

89. Which of the following is the most appropriate reason to use audio-visual materials in the classroom?
    a. To fill time when the teacher is not prepared for a class
    b. To give students additional insight into the forces that shaped the historical event you are studying.
    c. To fill time when a substitute will be teaching your class
    d. None of the above

90. Why did the United States originally get involved with Vietnam?
    a. To prevent the spread of Communism in Southeast Asia
    b. To aid France in its attempt to maintain its colonial presence in Vietnam.
    c. To prevent the overthrow of a pro-Western regime
    d. None of the above

91. Researching the history of levee building in the United States is most likely to also touch upon which of the following disciplines?
    I. Economics
    II. Geography
    III. Sociology
    a. I only
    b. II only
    c. I and II
    d. I and III

92. Which of the following is a purpose of a research question?
    a. To determine if one's topic can be researched
    b. To focus a broad research topic
    c. To evaluate your research topic
    d. None of the above

93. After reading the journals of several citizens of your home town, you find that several of them share the same opinions on a topic. In your paper, you infer that most of the population shared this opinion. What is this an example of?
    a. Using your sources to create a generalization
    b. Using your sources to identify a cause and effect relationship
    c. Finding a main idea
    d. All of the above

94. A historian is researching daily life in your home town in the 1840s. What might he do to locate sources?
    a. Contact descendants of people who lived in your town to see if they have any records
    b. Go to your home town's court house to see if land or court records are available.
    c. Go to your home town's library to see if they have information about the town's history
    d. All of the above

95. In which of the following circumstances would it be appropriate to use a chronological view to understand history?
    a. When discussing the role of religion in ancient civilizations
    b. When discussing cultural differences between civilizations in different climates
    c. When discussing the U.S.-Soviet race to the moon
    d. When looking at the role of families in various civilizations

96. In studying the causes of the crusades, which other academic discipline would be the least beneficial?
    a. Sociology
    b. Economics
    c. Literature
    d. Geography

97. Which of the following documents would be most appropriate to determine a historical figure's personal opinion on an event in which he was involved?
    a. A biography written by a close friend of him or her.
    b. The historical figure's personal journal
    c. A biography written by a noted historian with a related specialty
    d. Letters written by the historical figure's aide or assistant.

98. Which of the following are topics that should be covered in a high school (grades 9-12) U.S. history class?

    I. The Great Depression

    II. The Jacksonian Era Indian removal

    III. Cold War foreign policy

    IV. Progressive era reforms

    a. I, II, & III

    b. II & IV

    c. I, III & IV

    d. I & III

Constructed Response

The Great Depression was a sudden turning point for U.S. culture. Under President Franklin D. Roosevelt's "New Deal" legislation, programs and departments like the Works Progress Administration, Civilian Conservation Corps, Social Security System, and Securities and Exchange Commission, among others, were born. Discuss the impact the Great Depression and subsequent New Deal legislation had on U.S. history, focusing on how these effects can still be seen in the current culture, economy, and political ideology of the United States.

Answers and Explanations

1. C: The first great human civilization was the Sumerian civilization which was located in Mesopotamia. Mesopotamia encompasses the area between the Tigris and Euphrates Rivers in modern-day Iraq and is also referred to as "the Cradle of Civilization," and includes part of the Fertile Crescent.
The Sumerian civilization is credited with being the first to practice serious, year round agriculture. There is question over whether Sumeria or Ancient Egypt was the first to have a written language. Sumeria's writing began hieroglyphically and then developed into a form of writing known as cuneiform.

2. A: Anubis was the Egyptian god of the dead, typically depicted as being half human and half jackal.
Hatshepsut was an Egyptian queen who declared herself king while acting as regent for her stepson (who was also her son-in-law). She was the fifth pharaoh of Egypt's 18th dynasty Ramesses (or Ramses) II was the third pharaoh of Egypt's 19th Dynasty, and Egypt's greatest, most powerful and most celebrated pharaoh. He is also traditionally considered to be the pharaoh of the Bible's Book of Exodus. His tomb in the Valley of the Kings was discovered in 1881. Tutankhamen was the boy pharaoh whose tomb was found in 1922, intact and untouched by tomb raiders, leading to a surge of popular interest in ancient Egypt.

3. C: Pope Urban II's plan for an army made up of previously trained military personnel was thwarted by the popular excitement concerning the First Crusade. This led to the creation of large armies primarily made up of untrained, unskilled, undisciplined, and ill- or unequipped soldiers, most of whom were recruited from the poorest levels of society. These armies were the first to set forth on the Crusade, which became known as the People's Crusade. Even though some of these armies contained knights, they were ultimately ineffective as fighting forces. These armies were prone to rioting and raiding surrounding areas for food and supplies and were viewed as a destabilizing influence by local leaders. They were defeated in battle and many converted to Islam to avoid being killed.

4. A: Knights Templar is the name by which the Poor Fellow-Soldiers of Christ and of the Temple of Solomon is more commonly called. The Knights Templar began as a small and impoverished order intended to serve as a fighting force in the Holy Land, but soon grew into a large organization and a favorite charity. As the Templars' resources grew, their operations did and their activities included the management of an early form of banking that permitted travelers to carry less money with them, making the travelers a less tempting target for thieves and increasing their safety.

5. A: Mary Wollstonecraft wrote *A Vindication of the Rights of Woman* in the late eighteenth century in response to contemporary events and practices. Wollstonecraft called for equality in education at a time when many people believed that women only required domestic education that would enable them to run households.

The Declaration of Sentiments was a document addressing the rights of women; it was primarily written by Elizabeth Cady Stanton and then read to and signed by the delegates to the Seneca Falls Convention.

Frankenstein was written by Mary Wollstonecraft's daughter, Mary Wollstonecraft Shelley.

The Awakening was written by Kate Chopin and published in 1899.

6. B: The Dome of the Rock is the oldest existing Muslim structure and was built on the traditional site of Mohammed's ascent into heaven on Temple Mount. Before this, however, the Temple Mount was the site of the Jewish Second Temple which stood from the 6th Century BC until AD 70 when it was destroyed by Romans in response to a Jewish uprising in Jerusalem. The Temple Mount is also the traditional site of Solomon's Temple (also known as the First Temple) and its one remaining wall, known as the Western Wall or the Wailing Wall is an important Jewish shrine.

7. D: The Nile River was the lifeblood of the Ancient Egyptian Empire and is sometimes credited with being the reason this empire was able to become one of history's most stable societies. Its yearly floods replenished the soil by leaving fertile silt that made large scale agriculture possible in the land immediately surrounding the river. The agriculture provided Egypt with goods to trade, further enriching the empire. The Nile was also the center of Egyptian cultural and spiritual life. The ancient Egyptians believed that the pharaoh was responsible for providing the yearly floods as part of his role as the divinely appointed ruler.

8. B: The Mongol people have traditionally been nomads living in large white felt tents that are commonly known as "yurts" or "gers" and in Mongolia, many of these people still live in this traditional housing. The term yurt is of Turkish and Russian origins, while ger is the Mongolian term. The Mongol ger is designed, decorated and positioned based on a strict formula determined by religion, tradition, and superstition. Today the Mongol people are spread over the Asian steppe region including Mongolia, and parts of Russia, China Afghanistan and Pakistan.

9. C: The Sugar Act of 1764 raised import duties on goods which were not of British origin, including sugar, while reducing the import tax on molasses. The Stamp Act of 1765 was a tax of paper and printed products, intended to help the British government recoup some of the costs of the French and Indian War. It was extremely unpopular with the colonists and was repealed in 1766. Lead was one of the goods taxed under the Townshend Acts, enacted in 1767, but it did not receive its own specific tax act. The Tea Act of 1773 was another unpopular tax and led to tea boycotts and was the catalyst for the Boston Tea Party.

10. B: The Founding Fathers decided that because the colonies did not have the right to elect representatives to the British Parliament they could not be justly ruled by Parliament. They envisioned the British Empire's government as being headed by the King of England, under whom the various local parliaments and legislative bodies served to enact laws for the peoples whom they represented. By addressing their ills to the king, the Founding Fathers sought to prevent the appearance that they acknowledged the British Parliament in London as having any authority over the American colonies.

11. B: Marbury v. Madison started with the election of Thomas Jefferson as third President of the United States. The lame-duck Congress responded by issuing a large number of judicial patents, which the incoming president and Secretary of State refused to deliver to

their holders. Marbury, who was to receive a patent as Justice of the Peace, sued to demand delivery. What makes this case important is the decision which declared the judiciary's ability to overturn legislation that conflicted with the Constitution. The case states: "It is emphatically the province and duty of the judicial department to say what the law is. Those who apply the rule to particular cases must, of necessity, expound and interpret that rule. If two laws conflict with each other, the courts must decide on the operation of each.

"So if a law be in opposition to the Constitution; if both the law and the constitution apply to a particular case, so that the court must either decide that case conformably to the law, disregarding the Constitution; or conformably to the Constitution, disregarding the law; the court must determine which of these conflicting rules governs the case. This is of the very essence of judicial duty.

"If, then, the courts are to regard the Constitution, and the Constitution is superior to any ordinary act of the legislature, the Constitution, and not such ordinary act, must govern the case to which they both apply."

Later the ruling states: "The judicial power of the United States is extended to all cases arising under the Constitution." It was in this way that the Supreme Court achieved its now traditional ability to strike down laws and to act as the final arbitrator of what is and is not allowed under the U.S. Constitution.

12. D: Abraham Lincoln issued the Thanksgiving Proclamation on October 3, 1863, in which he specified the last Thursday of November as a day of thanksgiving. The last Thursday in November then became the traditional date for the Thanksgiving holiday as it is now celebrated in the United States.

During the Great Depression, President Roosevelt changed the holiday's date from the last Thursday in November to the fourth Thursday in November in order to stimulate the economy by creating a longer Christmas shopping season. This action met with some initial resistance but has since been accepted by the American people.

13. A: Historiography can be described as the study of the study of history. It is a term used to describe the entire body of historical literature, the writing of history and the critical examination of past historical writings and historical sources. A typical historiographic essay will be a critical look at the past historical research whether it is a broad look at the study of history as a whole or of a specific subject that is being analyzed.

14. B: The philosophy of history is concerned with the ultimate significance of history as a field of study and asks questions concerning how history should be studied, including what social unit is correct to use when studying history—whether it is more important to look at the individual lives of ordinary people or to concentrate on the so-called big picture, looking at the overall trends in a society or culture; only giving personal treatment to people, such as George Washington, who had particular significance to the events surrounding them. The philosophy of history also looks for broad historical trends and progress.

15. C: When researching historical events, the best sources are typically the earliest sources, particularly if they are primary sources written by witnesses soon after the event. While Wikipedia and your colleague's notes might be accurate, they are removed from the actual event and to you, their sources are thus in question.

The newspaper article and the wounded survivor's account are both good sources. Without knowing anything about the personal reliability of the authors, it is best to accept the survivor's account as it is both a personal, primary account and the earliest record available to you.

16. C: While wounds from war most certainly killed more than a few, European disease laid waste to vast swaths of Native American people who has no immunity to the foreign diseases which the Europeans carried. The forced marches took place in the mid-19th century under Andrew Jackson's presidency and are thus removed from the time frame in question.

17. C: The Dome of the Rock is the oldest existing Muslim structure, the shrine having been completed in AD 691. The rock in question is the traditional site for Mohammed's ascent into heaven accompanied by the angel Gabriel and documented in the Koran. The Dome of the Rock is a shrine for Muslim pilgrims and non-Muslims have commonly been barred from visiting the monument. The most recent ban lasted from 2000 to 2006. The religion of Islam was founded in Mecca, which is located in present-day Saudi Arabia.

18. D: Gutenberg's press used moveable metal type which he formed casting a metal alloy into molds made for each character. These individual pieces were then organized by letter. The letters were loaded into composing sticks that were then loaded into a metal form to create printing plates. As the printing press spread across Europe, printers began using woodcut prints to include illustrations in their products.
While Gutenberg is generally given credit for the invention of moveable type, in the 1040s Pi Sheng, a Chinese inventor and alchemist, created moveable type using clay characters which were then pressed into wax-coated plates for printing.

19. A: The U.S. Constitution, Article I, Section 3 states that: "The Senate of the United States shall be composed of two Senators from each state, chosen by the legislature thereof, for six years; and each Senator shall have one vote." This was the practice until the Seventeenth Amendment was ratified on April 8, 1913. The Seventeenth Amendment states that U.S. Senators are to be elected by the people of the states which they serve and that the state executive branches may appoint replacement Senators if a Senate seat becomes vacant mid-term, until the state legislature can arrange for a popular election.

20. B: The Erie Canal opened in 1825 and created a water route between the Hudson River and Lake Erie. Water routes have historically been cheaper and easier than overland ones and the Erie Canal was originally proposed in the 1700s as a means of providing a shipping route to assist in settling the areas west of the Appalachian Mountains.
The Mississippi River is to the west of the Great Lakes, its source is in Minnesota and it discharges into the Gulf of Mexico approximately 100 miles downstream of New Orleans, Louisiana.
The Susquehanna River runs through New York, Pennsylvania and Maryland and is the home of Three Mile Island, the site of the United States' largest nuclear disaster.
The Lehigh River is located in eastern Pennsylvania.

21. C: The telegraph was a gigantic leap forward in the realm of communications. Before the telegraph, messages could take days, weeks or months to reach their intended recipient, based upon the distance that they had to travel. The telegraph allowed people to send methods through use of electric signals transmitted over telegraph wires, allowing for instantaneous communications. The main drawbacks to the telegraph included the need to "translate" the message into and out of the appropriate telegraphic code and that the

- 110 -

telegraph could only relay one message at a time. In contrast, the telephone allowed for spoken communication between people at different locations, increasing the efficiency and speed as the people on each end of the conversation could communicate multiple messages quickly and in one telephone conversation.

22. A: The Incan civilization was very wealthy and the Incan rulers' individual wealth was used to care for their mummified remains following their deaths in order to emphasize the king's divinity as descendants of the Incan sun god Inti. When an Incan king died not only would his wealth be used to care for his remains, there would also be human sacrifices as the king's servants and favorite wives would be sacrificed so that they could continue serving him in the afterlife.

23. A: This picture was taken outside of the White House in 1918 and could be used to show students an example of a woman picketing as part of the fight to win the right to vote. In 1917, Alice Paul had begun organizing her followers into groups in order to picket the White House with signs intended to embarrass President Woodrow Wilson into supporting women's right to vote. These picketers did so at their own peril as many were arrested on charges of obstructing traffic. Those who were convicted served sentences at a local workhouse where they were subject to harsh conditions, including force-feedings.

24. D: Besides being Athens' primary marketplace, the Agora also served as a central point where ancient Athenians would go to meet friends, conduct business, discuss ideas and participate in local government. While most ancient Greek cities contained agorés, the Athenian Agora was particularly known for its intellectual opportunities. Socrates, Plato and Aristotle were all known to frequent the Athenian agora. The Athenian Agora is also credited with being the birthplace of democracy. The ancient Athenian democracy allowed all citizens the opportunity to vote on civic matters and serve on juries.

25. A: Genghis Khan, also spelled Chinggis Khan, was the son of a minor Mongol chieftain, born circa 1162 AD. His birth name was Temujin and he grew up in poverty, but gradually built his own power base to include a confederacy of Mongol clans. He was named Genghis Khan, or universal ruler, in 1206.
Attila the Hun was the 5th Century Hunnic leader who led his people to attack into Western Europe, going as far as Gaul (modern day France).
The leader of China's 19th Century Taiping Rebellion was Hong Xiuquan, also known as Hong Houxiu.

26. A: Bias is a form of prejudice, and a historical work is considered biased when it is unreasonably shaped by the author's personal or institutional prejudices. It is wise for a teacher to choose material that comes from reputable sources and to verify that all material used in classroom presentations is reliable and appropriate. As long as the teacher is willing to do these things and show a variety of historical opinions, this is not an example of bias.

27. D: Chronology can be defined as a list of events organized in order of their occurrence. An anachronism is a chronological error; something or someone who appears out of order chronologically. Anachronisms are frequently seen in popular entertainment dramatizations of historical events. Anno Domini is a Latin term meaning "in the year of [Our] Lord," more frequently seen as the abbreviation A.D. (e.g., "the Battle of Hastings was fought in A.D. 1066."). Chroma is a word used to describe color.

28. B: Sacagawea acted as Lewis and Clark's guide during their exploration of the Louisiana Purchase. She had been separated from her family at a young age and was reunited with her brother on the course of the expedition. Pocahontas was the daughter of Powhatan, the leader of the Algonquian tribes at the beginning of the 17th Century when the colony of Jamestown was founded in modern-day Virginia. Squanto's actual name was Tisquantum. He was the Native American who helped the Pilgrims after their first winter in Massachusetts. Wauwatosa is a suburb of Milwaukee, Wisconsin.

29. A: The idea behind Laissez faire was to leave the market alone and let it take care of itself with minimal government intervention. Opponents of this policy often blame it for causing the situation which led to the Great Depression while supporters claim that it was an increase of government interference in the market that led to the Great Depression. Social Darwinism is the idea that the fittest members of society will rise to the top and flourish.
Keynesian Economics advocates that the government should use its powers to stabilize the economy through raising and lowering interest rates and creating demand through government spending, frequently leading to deficit spending. Keynesian economic theory is chiefly concerned with microeconomic trends and short-term solutions. It's founder, John Maynard Keynes, was quoted saying, "[i]n the long run, we are all dead."
Monetarism is an economic school of thought that concentrates on macroeconomic principles and long-term solutions to economic problems. An economist supporting this policy would be in favor of policies that are monetarily neutral in the long term but are not neutral in the short term.

30. A: Lyndon Johnson became president following the assassination of John F. Kennedy on November 22, 1963. The Great Society was a series of social programs implemented under the direction of Lyndon Johnson. The Great Society's goal was to eliminate poverty and racial injustice in America. The Great Society began with economic reforms including a tax cut and the creation of the Office of Economic Opportunity. From there, it grew to include the enaction of laws creating the Medicare and Medicaid systems to assist the elderly and poor with their health care costs, respectively. Educational and Housing reforms followed.

31. C: Woodrow Wilson's Fourteen Points were set forth in a speech which he gave to a joint session of Congress on January 8, 1918, approximately 10 months before the end of World War I on November 11, 1918. These points set forth his plan for the rehabilitation of Germany and the creation of a lasting peace in Europe. They included adjustments of European borders, including the creation of an independent Polish state and allowing the peoples of Europe the benefits of self-determination.

32. B: Jamestown, Virginia was originally founded and settled by members of the Virginia Company of London, chartered by King James I of England. The Virginia Company was a profit-making venture and the first settlers of Jamestown were instructed to search for gold and a water route to Asia. Plymouth, Massachusetts was founded by the Pilgrims in 1620. Boston, Massachusetts was founded by the Puritans in 1630. The Pilgrims and Puritans were fleeing religious persecution in England. Providence, Rhode Island was founded in 1638 by followers of Roger Williams, a former Puritan leader, and his followers who had been exiled from Massachusetts due to their break with the Puritans.

33. D: Using maps to show post-World War II migration patterns or using charts and maps to illustrate the growth of U.S. cities would be examples of using appropriate visual aids in teaching history. Discussing the effects of weather on world history would be an example of connecting history with geography. Food shortages and inflation are both connected to economic conditions and discussing their destabilizing influence as a contributing factor to the Russian Revolution in 1917 would be an example of connecting history and economics.

34. C: The Great Depression began with the 1929 Stock Market Crash on Thursday, October 24, also known as Black Thursday. This crash was the beginning of a market collapse that continued as investors began panicking and banks began to fail.
The crash was due to rampant stock speculation and fraud. Many people had invested in the belief that the Stock Market could only go up, and unscrupulous people had taken advantage of this by creating sham companies or artificially pumping up stock shares. The SEC, or Securities and Exchange Commission, was created in 1934 to regulate stock exchanges.

35. B: The Pilgrims' initial intention had been to settle in Northern Virginia where England had already established a presence. As there was no government in place in New England, some Pilgrims believed that they had no legal or moral duty to remain with the Pilgrims' new colony which needed their labor and support. Because of this, the Mayflower Compact created a government in New England and was signed on board the Mayflower on November 11, 1620 by each of the adult men who made the journey.
The Compact's life was relatively short, due to its being superceded by the Pierce Patent in 1621 which had been signed by the king of England and had granted the Pilgrims the right of self-government in Plymouth. In spite of its short lifespan, the Mayflower Compact is credited with being North America's first constitution.

36. A: Manifest Destiny was the idea that the United States was intended by God to expand to fill North America. There were various ideas on what this meant, yet at minimum it was the belief that the United States should expand to the Pacific Ocean. At maximum, it was the belief that the United States should expand to fill North America and South America. The idea behind why the United States should expand through greater territorial acquisitions was to expand the American ideals of freedom, democracy and self-government.

37. B: The Marshall Plan was the popular name for the European Recovery Program, named after Secretary of State George C. Marshall. Marshall had originally proposed the Plan as a solution to the widespread inflation, unemployment, food shortages and general lack of resources following World War II in a commencement speech at Harvard University in 1947. As enacted, it was intended to provide a solution to these problems and to prevent the spread of communism by decreasing Soviet influence.

38. D: Early civilizations flourished alongside rivers such as the Nile in Egypt, the Euphrates in Mesopotamia, and the Yellow River in China. Besides providing the ancient settlers with a water source, these rivers also provided the land with the rich and fertile silt that the rivers deposited during their regular flooding cycles, making large scale agriculture possible for the ancient peoples.

39. C: The original Magna Carta, signed by King John on June 15, 1215, was meant to protect the rights and property of the few powerful families that topped the feudal system. Its primary purpose was to force King John to recognize the supremacy of ancient liberties, to

limit his ability to raise funds and to reassert the principle of due process. The majority of the English population at that time was mentioned only once, in a clause concerning the use of court-set fines to punish minor offences. The last clause, which created an enforcement council of tenants-in-chief and clergymen would have severely limited the king's power and introduced the policy of 'majority rule.' However, the time was not yet right for the introduction of majority rule. In September 1215, three months after the signing of the Magna Carta, Pope Innocent III, at John's urging, annulled the "shameful and demeaning agreement, forced upon the king by violence and fear." A civil war broke out over this, which ended when John died the following year, in October 1216.

40. C: Even though the Maya were one of the two cultures to develop an urban civilization in a rain forest, their culture was predominately based upon rural life. Cities were primarily used as religious centers while day-to-day life usually centered around farming in the surrounding rainforest. Due to the rainforest land's relative infertility, Mayans used slash and burn agriculture methods that required them to move to new farming plots every two to seven years. Under these conditions it took a large amount of land to support even one family.

41. B: The 95 Theses were part of a letter of protest that Martin Luther wrote to his archbishop in 1517, when Luther was a monk in the Catholic Church. These theses criticized church practices, particularly the practice of selling indulgences. Some sources claim Luther nailed this document to the door of the All Saint's Church in Wittenburg (located in modern-day Germany). Luther's intention was to reform the Catholic Church from within, but his letter soon placed him at the center of a religious and civil revolt. He was excommunicated in 1520.

42. C: Alexander Hamilton was the Founding Father who is credited with founding the Federalist Party. Hamilton was a proponent of the idea that the young country required the support of the rich and powerful in order to survive. This party grew out of Hamilton's political connections in Washington and was particularly popular in the northeastern United States. John Adams was a member of this party. George Washington's personal beliefs were most closely aligned with the Federalist Party, but he disliked political parties and refused to become a member of one.
Thomas Jefferson was the founder of the Democratic-Republican Party.

43. B: The Shoguns were Japanese military leaders. During the Tokuwaga shogunate, which began in 1603, the shogun held the actual power in the Japanese government even though Japan was technically ruled by an emperor. In actuality, the emperor was primarily a ceremonial leader and access to him was restricted to members of the shogun's family.

44. D: The Iroquois Confederacy was a participatory democracy made up of Native American tribes in what is now the Northeastern United States. Each of the member tribes were permitted to send male representatives selected by the tribe's female members to the Confederacy's main counsel where each representative was permitted to vote on matters affecting the tribes. The beginnings of the Iroquois Confederacy are disputed, but it is accepted that the Confederacy was originally made up of the Mohawk, Seneca, Onondaga, Cayuga, and Oneida tribes; the Tuscaroras joined the Confederacy in 1722. The Confederacy was formed with the intention of decreasing intertribal violence and encouraging peaceful resolution of differences between the tribes.

45. B: James Oglethorpe was a philanthropist who wanted to give England's "worthy poor" the opportunity to prosper away from the highly stratified class structure in England. The original idea was to include people released from debtors' prison among the colonists, though none of the original 114 colonists were debtors just released. Oglethorpe's intention was to create a classless society so that Georgia would not develop the same problems that had plagued England. Oglethorpe was one of the original colonists, even though the colonial charter prohibited him from profiting from the colony and was frequently referred to as the colony's "resident trustee."

46. A: The historical evidence shows that the initial workers on tobacco plantations in Virginia were primarily indentured servants who would eventually receive their freedom. The path to slavery in its later forms was gradual, beginning with slavery as a form of punishment for legal infractions. Massachusetts became the first colony to legalize slavery in 1641, followed by other states, including Virginia. This was followed by laws declaring that any children born to a slave mother would be slaves themselves in 1662 and a later decision that all persons who were not Christians in their "native country" would be slaves in 1705.

47. C: The term Five Civilized Tribes came into use during the middle of the 19th Century as a means of referring to the Creek, Cherokee, Choctaw, Chickasaw, and Seminole tribes, each of whom had developed complex social and government systems including written constitutions, judicial, legislative and executive systems, complex agriculture practices and the establishment of public schools.

48. A: In 50 BC, Julius Caesar was called back to Rome by the Roman Senate in order to stand trial for treason and corruption. When he reached the Rubicon, he decided to ignore Roman Law and the Mos Maiorum (uncodified tradition with nearly the force of law), and instead took one legion to Rome with him, famously uttering the words "the die is cast." This was the beginning of a chain of events that led to the creation of the first Roman triumvirate and the transition of Rome from a Republic to an Empire, with Julius Caesar as "Perpetual Dictator," until his murder in the Senate. His adopted son Octavius (later taking the regnal name "Augustus") eventually became the first emperor.

49. B: Edward Jenner's initial smallpox vaccine was comprised of liquid from a young milkmaid's cowpox sores. Jenner was a country doctor who had noticed that persons who had suffered from the relatively mild disease of cowpox did not later catch the much more serious and deadly smallpox. At this time, the main preventative measure against smallpox was to inoculate healthy people with the liquid from smallpox sores from those who had mild cases of smallpox. Unfortunately, this practice often lead to healthy people having full blown cases of smallpox that resulted in death. Jenner's belief was that if he could inoculate someone with the liquid from cowpox pustules, they would then be immune from smallpox without the risk of contracting a full case of smallpox. In May 1796, Jenner diagnosed a patient, a milkmaid named Sarah Nelmes, with cowpox and received permission from a local farmer to inoculate the farmer's son James with cowpox, and then expose him to smallpox. Jenner made two cuts on James's arms and poured liquid from Sarah Nelmes's sores on them before binding the wound. James came down with a mild case of cowpox six weeks later, after James was well again, Jenner exposed him to smallpox, which the young boy did not contract. Jenner conducted further tests and in 1798 he published his findings in a report which introduced the words vaccination (adapted from the Latin word for cow).

50. A: Hiroshima had an atom bomb detonated over it on August 6, 1945, officially beginning the atomic age; Nagasaki was bombed three days later. Both cities were selected for atomic bombing because they had not been previously bombed during the war.

51. A: Feudalism was a common practice during the Middle Ages, popular as a means of providing social structure and for maintaining the established government and social order. It was most widespread and systemic in Europe but also practiced in other parts of the world including Persia and the Byzantine Empire.

The Norsemen of what is now known as Scandinavia, however, were an exception to European feudalism and lived in a fairly egalitarian society where rank was strongly based on personal merit. This is not to say that the Norsemen were entirely opposed to the class delineations of feudalism; when the French King Charles the Simple ceded to them the land that became the province of Normandy, the Norsemen who settled there settled into a feudalistic structure that their descendants took with them to England during the Norman Conquest, where the feudal system was used to assist with subduing the newly-conquered English people.

52. C: The passage describes the reasons why the Constitution has managed to last for over two hundred years and would be an appropriate part of an essay answering question C. It might also be an appropriate part of an essay answering questions A or B, but because this passage directly deals with the Constitution's longevity C is the best answer. The Federalist Party was a distinct group from the Federalists who supported the ratification of the Constitution.

53. D: The passage could be best used to describe the attributes of the U.S. Constitution in a government class. The passage does not go in-depth into the formation of the Constitution, the basis of U.S. law or why the U.S. Constitution can be amended.

54. B: The passage describes the reasons the U.S. Constitution has survived for so long, including the fact that it provides a set of basic rules but allows amendment so that it can be altered as new situations arise.

55. C: The people who were opposed to the idea of having a bill of rights in the Constitution were primarily concerned that by specifically enumerating a set of rights, that there would be an argument that the rights not listed did not exist or were not important.
The Bill of Rights did not initially apply to the states even though there was some concern that the states were more likely to infringe upon individual liberties than the federal government.

56. C: The Federalist Papers were written and published anonymously by John Jay, Alexander Hamilton, and James Madison as part of their effort to ratify the Constitution. There are 85 letters in total and they were meant to convince normal Americans that they should support the Constitution by explaining what it meant and what it was intended to accomplish.

57. D: The New Deal met with conservative opposition, especially in the Supreme Court, whose conservative justices frequently blocked New Deal legislation. The plan that was dubbed the "court packing" plan was to appoint a second justice for every justice over the age of seventy. Because all of the conservative justices on the Supreme Court were over

seventy, this would have given Roosevelt the ability to appoint enough justices to swing the Court to his favor. However, this plan was met with extreme popular disapproval which led to its eventual abandonment.

58. D: Eli Whitney's cotton engine (or gin) was designed to aid in the cleaning of American cotton. Before this invention, cleaning American short-staple cotton was a long and tedious process as all the cotton seeds had to be removed from the cotton by hand, usually by slaves. Whitney's invention could clean more cotton than an individual person could, thereby increasing cotton's profitability and turning it into a cash crop. As cotton became a viable cash crop, the amount of land dedicated to its cultivation increased, as well as the number of laborers needed to work in the cotton fields, which resulted in an overall increase in the number of slaves held in the southern United States. As cotton production increased, cotton also became a major Southern export as textile mills in both the northern United States and Europe became dependant on Southern cotton.

59. B: The Sherman Anti-Trust Act of 1890 was enacted in response to the growth of large monopolies in the period following the end of the Civil War. While its purpose was to prevent restraints on free trade, it was not strictly enforced. Additionally, the wording was vague enough that it was also used to break up labor unions. It was replaced by the Clayton Antitrust Act in 1914.

60. C: The U.S. Supreme Court justices had decided that *Brown* would have a unanimous holding (the legal term for a court's rulings or decisions) before they determined what that holding would be, which resulted in a fairly narrow holding that "the plaintiffs and others similarly situated for whom the actions have been brought are, by reason of the segregation complained of, deprived of the equal protection of the laws guaranteed by the Fourteenth Amendment." This decision was used in later Civil Rights cases as a legal precedent for the idea that the doctrine of "separate but equal" was inherently unconstitutional, reversing the precedent set by *Plessy v. Ferguson*.

61. D: The French Revolution began in 1789, but its end date has been difficult to define. The Reign of Terror was intended as a means of fighting the revolutionaries' enemies and began with the execution of the Queen Marie Antoinette on October 17, 1793. While there was an economic crisis leading up to the French Revolution, there was also a severe economic crisis during/following the Revolution (depending on one's preferred end date). One of the effects of the Revolution was the ending of feudalism and slavery in France. With regard to the Estates-General, King Louis XVI had called together the Estates-General on August 8, 1788, stated that the Estates General would convene in May 1789.

62. A: Under the rule of the shoguns, Japan was primarily a closed country; contact with outsiders was severely limited. As a general rule, outsiders who attempted to go to Japan were killed, as were Japanese people who attempted to leave. The primarily exceptions to this rule were Chinese and Dutch traders who were granted permission to trade with the Japanese people. This situation changed in 1854 when the United States and Japan entered into a treaty of permanent friendship following U.S. Commodore Matthew Perry's entry into what is now Tokyo Bay Harbor in 1853 (albeit with an armed fleet).

63. B: The Articles of Confederation granted the federal Congress the power to enter into treaties. It did not grant Congress the abilities to collect taxes, enforce laws or to regulate interstate commerce (it could impose some regulations on commerce with foreign entities),

these shortcomings led to the eventual abandonment of the Articles of Confederation in favor of the Constitution, which is still in force today.

64. A: In *The Republic*, Plato calls for a philosopher king, selected from the ranks of philosophers who are at least fifty years old and given the power of absolute rule for life. Plato's belief was that in this society there should be no laws as they would interfere with the king's ability to use his judgment.

65. C: The Neolithic agricultural revolution resulted in an overall decrease in leisure time, in comparison with people living in hunter-gatherer societies, due to such factors as sustaining an increased standard of living and caring for the increased number of children born to families living in permanent settlements.

66. C: The 26th Amendment states: "The right of citizens of the United States, who are 18 years of age or older, to vote, shall not be denied or abridged by the United States or any state on account of age. " The 24th Amendment invalidates poll taxes as a requirement to vote. The 25th Amendment deals with presidential succession. The 27th Amendment deals with Congress members' compensation.

67. B: Mountains provide societies with a natural protective barrier, making it difficult for an outside force to invade them. The Swiss Alps are frequently credited with being a reason that Switzerland has managed to maintain its independence and neutrality. The barrier created by the mountains can also discourage trade and prevent cultural diffusion.

68. C: The principles held in the Monroe Doctrine were not new when President James Monroe issued it in a speech before Congress on December 2, 1823, however that did not stop them from becoming his namesake and shaping American foreign policy, even through the World Wars to which the U.S. remained aloof until threatened with attack in the Western Hemisphere. Germany's attempt to convince Mexico to attack the United States, promising Mexico that it would receive several U.S. states as a reward, was one of the issues that convinced the U.S. to intervene in what had hitherto been seen as a European war. In World War II, the United States remained officially neutral until attacked at Pearl Harbor. The Monroe Doctrine was largely ignored by European powers, but underscored the American belief that the United States was the appropriate dominant power in the Western Hemisphere.

69. D: Nelson Mandela was the first President of South Africa to be elected in a fully representative South African election. He was succeeded by Thabo Mbeki, who was succeeded by Kgalema Motlanthe. Mahatma Gandhi was an Indian who lived in South Africa for a time and greatly influenced Nelson Mandela. He was also the leader of India's independence movement.

70. B: On June 28, 1914, Archduke Franz Ferdinand and his wife the Duchess Sophia von Chotkova were assassinated by Gavrilo Princip, a member of The Black Hand, a secret society whose intention was to create an independent Serbian country. This act was the first of a series of events that resulted in the beginning of World War later that summer. The Japanese bombed Pearl Harbor on December 7, 1941, bringing the United States into World War II.

The sinking of the RMS *Lusitania* and the British interception of the Zimmerman telegram, in which Germany attempted to encourage Mexico to attack the United States, led to the United States entering World War I in 1917.

71. A: Boris Yeltsin was a Russian politician who was instrumental in the breaking up of the USSR and the end of Communism in Russia. In 1991, he was elected President of the Russian Federation in Russia's first democratic election.

72. C: This was almost a direct quote from President Truman's 1947 address before Congress which later became known The Truman Doctrine. The address explained his reasoning as to why the United States needed to offer assistance to Greece and Turkey.

73. B: The Warsaw Treaty Organization was meant to counterbalance NATO, or the North Atlantic Treaty Organization. Members of NATO included the United States, Great Britain, France and West Germany and pledged to consider an attack on one of them as an attack on all of them.
NAFTA (the North American Free Trade Agreement) was signed by President Clinton in 1994 and lifted most trade barriers between the United States, Mexico and, Canada.
The Soviet Union was a member of the U.N. Security Counsel which is charged with maintaining international Peace and Security.
The Four Power Pact was a pre-World War II treaty in which the United States, Great Britain, Japan and France agreed to respect each other's Pacific territories.

74. D: At the beginning of the Civil War, the Confederacy drew many skilled officers such as Robert E. Lee out of the Union army and used them as the backbone of its military leadership. The Union Army, meanwhile, went through a series of unsatisfactory generals before Lincoln found Ulysses S. Grant. The other options were advantages that the North held over the South.

75. D: The Mormon pioneers were members of The Church of Jesus Christ of Latter-day Saints and their trek west was intended to transport their entire culture across the plains to a place where they would be safe from the persecutions they had suffered in their previous settlements, including Missouri's Extermination Order (1838) and the assassination of the church's leader, Joseph Smith, on June 27, 1844 in Carthage, Illinois, while under the protection of Illinois' governor.
In moving their culture across the Plains, the Mormons not only moved the people but took care to bring religious and secular books and musical instruments on their thousand mile journey. One of the first buildings in Salt Lake City was a theater. On the trek west, the Mormons divided themselves into highly organized companies and worked to improve the trail and provide resources for those coming after them, including the building of way stations, ferries and the planting of crops. They also kept detailed records of their experiences for the use of future pioneers, and an early Mormon pioneer invented the odometer as a means of calculating how far his company had traveled each day. Their migration is the most highly organized mass migration in U.S. history.

76. B: The New Deal did not end the Depression. The Depression only ended after the beginning of World War II when there was a huge increase in demand for goods and manpower. The New Deal increased the agricultural price supports offered to farmers and increased the role that the federal government played in the U.S. economy.

77. A: Cesar Chavez was a migrant farm worker who founded the United Farm Workers Organizing Committee. He was instrumental in bringing about several reforms that improved living and working conditions for migrant workers including the banning of certain grape pesticides and of the short handled hoe used in lettuce harvesting.

78. C: While Civil Rights Era Supreme Court decisions did declare that segregation in schools violated the equal protection clause of the Constitution, these decisions did not lead to instantaneous desegregation of schools, as people in many locations resisted desegregation even going to the length of closing public schools to prevent it. In other areas the National Guard had to be called in to enforce orders to integrate the schools.

79. D: The industrialization of the United States led to an overall decrease in the number of farmers as people moved from the country to the city in search of the new jobs created by industrialization. This move also resulted in fewer Americans being self-employed, as they instead became wage earners working for other people.
Industrialization also led to an overall increase in economic and employment opportunities for women. Many of these opportunities took the form of what we now sometimes think of as "pink collar" jobs such as typing and stenography.

80. C: The Dust Bowl was a period of time, largely coinciding with the Great Depression, in which severe droughts, poor farming techniques, wind erosion and several other factors led to the collapse of farming in the southern Plains states. High grain prices had encouraged farmers to over-cultivate their fields and to bring previously uncultivated land under cultivation, leading to soil depletion and an overall loss in soil moisture as farmers would frequently burn their wheat stubble. This was a problem because the long grasses in the Plains states had previously been instrumental in keeping the soil in place. This loss meant that windstorms now began picking up soil, eroding fields and destroying crops.
The Dust Bowl resulted in thousands of farmers losing their farms. Many of them traveled to California where they worked as migrant farm workers. John Steinbeck's The Grapes of Wrath tells the story of one family who lost their farm in Oklahoma due to the Dust Bowl.

81. A: The Enlightenment, also known as The Age of Enlightenment and The Age of Reason, occurred in the eighteenth century and centered on a belief in reason. The Enlightenment encouraged the ideals of liberty, self-governance, natural rights and natural law. Both the American Revolution and the French Revolution had their genesis in Enlightenment ideals which encouraged the idea that the common man should have a say in government. This was a departure from the most common types of governance, including monarchy and the belief in the divine right of kings. Enlightenment leaders tended to prefer representative republics as a form of government.

82. D: The Hudson River School was the first well-known American school of painting. Its members intended to break away from the European art schools and develop a distinct American art school of thought through their celebration of the American landscape.

83. B: The Communist Manifesto claims that history has been a series of class struggles; that the rise of Communism will eliminate class boundaries and end the struggle. Karl Marx, the Manifesto's primary author, ended with a call for the working class of the world to start a revolution against the order of things, forcibly taking over the means of production. The final lines read:

"The Communists disdain to conceal their views and aims. They openly declare that their ends can be attained only by the forcible overthrow of all existing social conditions. Let the ruling classes tremble at a Communist revolution. The proletarians have nothing to lose but their chains. They have a world to win. Workingmen of all countries, unite!"

84. B: In a pure market economy, price is typically seen as a reflection of supply and demand. A larger supply will result in a lower price and a greater demand will result in a lower price.

85. C: The Internet has increased the number of methods in which near-instantaneous communication is possible, but this is not necessarily an economic spur. The internet has also generally caused a decrease in transaction costs and barriers to entry in retail situations (e.g., it is much less expensive to start a website to sell your goods than it is to open a brick and mortar store. Ones website has the potential to reach out to a much larger group of potential consumers). The Internet has also increased consumer access to goods by making it easier for consumers to locate what they want.

86. D: All of the answers are ways in which the Nazi government attempted to gain control of German children.

87. A: John Locke was an English philosopher aligned with the Whig party. He wrote his Two Treatises on Government in support of the Glorious Revolution which occurred when William of Orange took over the throne from James II in 1688-89.

88. D: The information in this table shows the median incomes of persons who have achieved various educational levels. Looking at the table, one can see that from 1997 to 2007, persons without a high school degree had their median income increase by less than $5,000 while persons with a high school degree had their median income increase by more than $6,000. One can also see that as a general matter, the more education a person has, the higher their income will be and that income typically increases over time.

89. B: The most appropriate reason listed in the question is to give students additional insight into the forces that shaped the historical event they are studying. Audio-visual materials can be used to give students additional perspective; for example, a documentary about the Battle of Gettysburg could be used to provide them with visual representations of historical locations or as a means of illustrating the differences in perspective.

90. B: Following World War II, European powers found themselves in a position where they faced resistance to their colonial rule at a time when they lacked the resources to maintain their presence by force. After France was defeated in Vietnam, the United States remained for reasons that included the two listed in A and C.

91. B: Levees are built to prevent flooding in areas along rivers. They consist of large embankments along the side of a river and typically have a flat top atop which sandbags can be piled to increase the levees' height when necessary. The Mississippi River has one of the world's largest levee systems.

92. B: A research question can be used to focus a research topic that is too broad to be appropriately handled in the format for which one is researching.

93. A: In this situation, you are using the information you have to create a generalization about the opinions of the population.

94. D: All of the listed methods are ways that a historian might locate sources, depending on his actual research question.

95. C: The U.S.-Soviet race to the moon is an example of a circumstance where a chronological point of view would be appropriate as each nation's advances fuelled the other nation's desire to surpass its Cold War rival.

96. C: Literature, while it may have described the crusades after the fact, would not be useful in determining the causes of them. Pope Urban II called the First Crusade at the Council of Clermont in November of 1095. This was primarily in response to three stimuli:
1) Constantinople, the centre of late-Roman, post-Roman and dark-age culture—and a major trading city—was being pressured militarily by the Muslim Seljuk Turks.
2) Christian feudal Europe was teeming with young men, desperate to prove their honor and valor according to the newly-developing code of honor that would shape the middle ages. A move to war would allay the inter- and intra-national squabbling, which was currently taking place throughout Europe, amongst Christians.
3) A new and dangerous religion had come to control Jerusalem, which the Church and Christian Europe saw as their own right.

Therefore, sociology would describe reason 2), a decision based upon sociological factors, such as unemployed youth, ready for war. Geography, combined with economics, would help explain the critical nature of the city of Constantinople, in that it controlled the Bosporus, the waterway between the Mediterranean and Black seas, and thus was the primary non-sea route to the Middle-East). For the crusaders, were it to fall, Muslims would control trade with the East even further, and the heart of Eastern Christianity would be lost.

97. B: The personal journal is the best source in this case because it is the only primary source listed. While a close friend's biography or an aide's letters might include information on the historical figure's personal opinion, the information will be filtered through the other person's memory and personal opinions.

98. C: High school U.S. History classes are intended to cover the history of the United States since Reconstruction. The Great Depression, The Cold War, and the Progressive Era all occurred following reconstruction. The Jacksonian era took place during Andrew Jackson's presidency which lasted from 1829 to 1837.

Secret Key #1 - Time is Your Greatest Enemy

Pace Yourself

Wear a watch. At the beginning of the test, check the time (or start a chronometer on your watch to count the minutes), and check the time after every few questions to make sure you are "on schedule."

If you are forced to speed up, do it efficiently. Usually one or more answer choices can be eliminated without too much difficulty. Above all, don't panic. Don't speed up and just begin guessing at random choices. By pacing yourself, and continually monitoring your progress against your watch, you will always know exactly how far ahead or behind you are with your available time. If you find that you are one minute behind on the test, don't skip one question without spending any time on it, just to catch back up. Take 15 fewer seconds on the next four questions, and after four questions you'll have caught back up. Once you catch back up, you can continue working each problem at your normal pace.

Furthermore, don't dwell on the problems that you were rushed on. If a problem was taking up too much time and you made a hurried guess, it must be difficult. The difficult questions are the ones you are most likely to miss anyway, so it isn't a big loss. It is better to end with more time than you need than to run out of time.

Lastly, sometimes it is beneficial to slow down if you are constantly getting ahead of time. You are always more likely to catch a careless mistake by working more slowly than quickly, and among very high-scoring test takers (those who are likely to have lots of time left over), careless errors affect the score more than mastery of material.

Secret Key #2 - Guessing is not Guesswork

You probably know that guessing is a good idea - unlike other standardized tests, there is no penalty for getting a wrong answer. Even if you have no idea about a question, you still have a 20-25% chance of getting it right.

Most test takers do not understand the impact that proper guessing can have on their score. Unless you score extremely high, guessing will significantly contribute to your final score.

Monkeys Take the Test

What most test takers don't realize is that to insure that 20-25% chance, you have to guess randomly. If you put 20 monkeys in a room to take this test, assuming they answered once per question and behaved themselves, on average they would get 20-25% of the questions correct. Put 20 test takers in the room, and the average will be much lower among guessed questions. Why?

1. The test writers intentionally writes deceptive answer choices that "look" right. A test taker has no idea about a question, so picks the "best looking" answer, which is often wrong. The monkey has no idea what looks good and what doesn't, so will consistently be lucky about 20-25% of the time.
2. Test takers will eliminate answer choices from the guessing pool based on a hunch or intuition. Simple but correct answers often get excluded, leaving a 0% chance of being correct. The monkey has no clue, and often gets lucky with the best choice.

This is why the process of elimination endorsed by most test courses is flawed and detrimental to your performance- test takers don't guess, they make an ignorant stab in the dark that is usually worse than random.

$5 Challenge

Let me introduce one of the most valuable ideas of this course- the $5 challenge:

You only mark your "best guess" if you are willing to bet $5 on it.
You only eliminate choices from guessing if you are willing to bet $5 on it.

Why $5? Five dollars is an amount of money that is small yet not insignificant, and can really add up fast (20 questions could cost you $100). Likewise, each answer choice on one question of the test will have a small impact on your overall score, but it can really add up to a lot of points in the end.

The process of elimination IS valuable. The following shows your chance of guessing it right:

If you eliminate wrong answer choices until only this many remain:	1	2	3
Chance of getting it correct:	100%	50%	33%

However, if you accidentally eliminate the right answer or go on a hunch for an incorrect answer, your chances drop dramatically: to 0%. By guessing among all the answer choices, you are GUARANTEED to have a shot at the right answer.

That's why the $5 test is so valuable- if you give up the advantage and safety of a pure guess, it had better be worth the risk.

What we still haven't covered is how to be sure that whatever guess you make is truly random. Here's the easiest way:

Always pick the first answer choice among those remaining.

Such a technique means that you have decided, **before you see a single test question**, exactly how you are going to guess- and since the order of choices tells you nothing about which one is correct, this guessing technique is perfectly random.

This section is not meant to scare you away from making educated guesses or eliminating choices- you just need to define when a choice is worth eliminating. The $5 test, along with a pre-defined random guessing strategy, is the best way to make sure you reap all of the benefits of guessing.

Secret Key #3 - Practice Smarter, Not Harder

Many test takers delay the test preparation process because they dread the awful amounts of practice time they think necessary to succeed on the test. We have refined an effective method that will take you only a fraction of the time.

There are a number of "obstacles" in your way to succeed. Among these are answering questions, finishing in time, and mastering test-taking strategies. All must be executed on the day of the test at peak performance, or your score will suffer. The test is a mental marathon that has a large impact on your future.

Just like a marathon runner, it is important to work your way up to the full challenge. So first you just worry about questions, and then time, and finally strategy:

Success Strategy

1. Find a good source for practice tests.
2. If you are willing to make a larger time investment, consider using more than one study guide- often the different approaches of multiple authors will help you "get" difficult concepts.
3. Take a practice test with no time constraints, with all study helps "open book." Take your time with questions and focus on applying strategies.
4. Take a practice test with time constraints, with all guides "open book."
5. Take a final practice test with no open material and time limits

If you have time to take more practice tests, just repeat step 5. By gradually exposing yourself to the full rigors of the test environment, you will condition your mind to the stress of test day and maximize your success.

Secret Key #4 - Prepare, Don't Procrastinate

Let me state an obvious fact: if you take the test three times, you will get three different scores. This is due to the way you feel on test day, the level of preparedness you have, and, despite the test writers' claims to the contrary, some tests WILL be easier for you than others.

Since your future depends so much on your score, you should maximize your chances of success. In order to maximize the likelihood of success, you've got to prepare in advance. This means taking practice tests and spending time learning the information and test taking strategies you will need to succeed.

Never take the test as a "practice" test, expecting that you can just take it again if you need to. Feel free to take sample tests on your own, but when you go to take the official test, be prepared, be focused, and do your best the first time!

Secret Key #5 - Test Yourself

Everyone knows that time is money. There is no need to spend too much of your time or too little of your time preparing for the test. You should only spend as much of your precious time preparing as is necessary for you to get the score you need.

Once you have taken a practice test under real conditions of time constraints, then you will know if you are ready for the test or not.

If you have scored extremely high the first time that you take the practice test, then there is not much point in spending countless hours studying. You are already there.

Benchmark your abilities by retaking practice tests and seeing how much you have improved. Once you score high enough to guarantee success, then you are ready.

If you have scored well below where you need, then knuckle down and begin studying in earnest. Check your improvement regularly through the use of practice tests under real conditions. Above all, don't worry, panic, or give up. The key is perseverance!

Then, when you go to take the test, remain confident and remember how well you did on the practice tests. If you can score high enough on a practice test, then you can do the same on the real thing.

General Strategies

The most important thing you can do is to ignore your fears and jump into the test immediately- do not be overwhelmed by any strange-sounding terms. You have to jump into the test like jumping into a pool- all at once is the easiest way.

Make Predictions

As you read and understand the question, try to guess what the answer will be. Remember that several of the answer choices are wrong, and once you begin reading them, your mind will immediately become cluttered with answer choices designed to throw you off. Your mind is typically the most focused immediately after you have read the question and digested its contents. If you can, try to predict what the correct answer will be. You may be surprised at what you can predict.

Quickly scan the choices and see if your prediction is in the listed answer choices. If it is, then you can be quite confident that you have the right answer. It still won't hurt to check the other answer choices, but most of the time, you've got it!

Answer the Question

It may seem obvious to only pick answer choices that answer the question, but the test writers can create some excellent answer choices that are wrong. Don't pick an answer just because it sounds right, or you believe it to be true. It MUST answer the question. Once you've made your selection, always go back and check it against the question and make sure that you didn't misread the question, and the answer choice does answer the question posed.

Benchmark

After you read the first answer choice, decide if you think it sounds correct or not. If it doesn't, move on to the next answer choice. If it does, mentally mark that answer choice. This doesn't mean that you've definitely selected it as your answer choice, it just means that it's the best you've seen thus far. Go ahead and read the next choice. If the next choice is worse than the one you've already selected, keep going to the next answer choice. If the next choice is better than the choice you've already selected, mentally mark the new answer choice as your best guess.

The first answer choice that you select becomes your standard. Every other answer choice must be benchmarked against that standard. That choice is correct until proven otherwise by another answer choice beating it out. Once you've decided that no other answer choice seems as good, do one final check to ensure that your answer choice answers the question posed.

Valid Information

Don't discount any of the information provided in the question. Every piece of information may be necessary to determine the correct answer. None of the information in the question is there to throw you off (while the answer choices will certainly have information to throw you off). If two seemingly unrelated topics are discussed, don't ignore either. You can be confident there is a relationship, or it wouldn't be included in the question, and you are probably going to have to determine what is that relationship to find the answer.

Avoid "Fact Traps"

Don't get distracted by a choice that is factually true. Your search is for the answer that answers the question. Stay focused and don't fall for an answer that is true but incorrect. Always go back to the question and make sure you're choosing an answer that actually answers the question and is not just a true statement. An answer can be factually correct, but it MUST answer the question asked. Additionally, two answers can both be seemingly correct, so be sure to read all of the answer choices, and make sure that you get the one that BEST answers the question.

Milk the Question

Some of the questions may throw you completely off. They might deal with a subject you have not been exposed to, or one that you haven't reviewed in years. While your lack of knowledge about the subject will be a hindrance, the question itself can give you many clues that will help you find the correct answer. Read the question carefully and look for clues. Watch particularly for adjectives and nouns describing difficult terms or words that you don't recognize. Regardless of if you completely understand a word or not, replacing it with a synonym either provided or one you more familiar with may help you to understand what the questions are asking. Rather than wracking your mind about specific detailed information concerning a difficult term or word, try to use mental substitutes that are easier to understand.

The Trap of Familiarity

Don't just choose a word because you recognize it. On difficult questions, you may not recognize a number of words in the answer choices. The test writers don't put "make-believe" words on the test; so don't think that just because you only recognize all the words in one answer choice means that answer choice must be correct. If you only recognize words in one answer choice, then focus on that one. Is it correct? Try your best to determine if it is correct. If it is, that is great, but if it doesn't, eliminate it. Each word and answer choice you eliminate increases your chances of getting the question correct, even if you then have to guess among the unfamiliar choices.

Eliminate Answers

Eliminate choices as soon as you realize they are wrong. But be careful! Make sure you consider all of the possible answer choices. Just because one appears right, doesn't mean that the next one won't be even better! The test writers will usually put more than one good answer choice for every question, so read all of them. Don't worry if you are stuck between two that seem right. By getting down to just two remaining possible choices, your odds are now 50/50. Rather than wasting too much time, play the odds. You are guessing, but guessing wisely, because you've been able to knock out some of the answer choices that you know are wrong. If you are eliminating choices and realize that the last answer choice you are left with is also obviously wrong, don't panic. Start over and consider each choice again. There may easily be something that you missed the first time and will realize on the second pass.

Tough Questions

If you are stumped on a problem or it appears too hard or too difficult, don't waste time. Move on! Remember though, if you can quickly check for obviously incorrect answer choices, your chances of guessing correctly are greatly improved. Before you completely give up, at least try to knock out a couple of possible answers. Eliminate what you can and then guess at the remaining answer choices before moving on.

Brainstorm

If you get stuck on a difficult question, spend a few seconds quickly brainstorming. Run through the complete list of possible answer choices. Look at each choice and ask yourself, "Could this answer the question satisfactorily?" Go through each answer choice and consider it independently of the other. By systematically going through all possibilities, you may find something that you would otherwise overlook. Remember that when you get stuck, it's important to try to keep moving.

Read Carefully

Understand the problem. Read the question and answer choices carefully. Don't miss the question because you misread the terms. You have plenty of time to read each question thoroughly and make sure you understand what is being asked. Yet a happy medium must be attained, so don't waste too much time. You must read carefully, but efficiently.

Face Value

When in doubt, use common sense. Always accept the situation in the problem at face value. Don't read too much into it. These problems will not require you to make huge leaps of logic. The test writers aren't trying to throw you off with a cheap trick. If you have to go beyond creativity and make a leap of logic in order to have an answer choice answer the question, then you should look at the other answer choices. Don't overcomplicate the problem by creating theoretical relationships or explanations that will warp time or space. These are normal problems rooted in reality. It's just that the applicable relationship or explanation may not be readily apparent and you have to figure things out. Use your common sense to interpret anything that isn't clear.

Prefixes

If you're having trouble with a word in the question or answer choices, try dissecting it. Take advantage of every clue that the word might include. Prefixes and suffixes can be a huge help. Usually they allow you to determine a basic meaning. Pre- means before, post- means after, pro - is positive, de- is negative. From these prefixes and suffixes, you can get an idea of the general meaning of the word and try to put it into context. Beware though of any traps. Just because con is the opposite of pro, doesn't necessarily mean congress is the opposite of progress!

Hedge Phrases

Watch out for critical "hedge" phrases, such as likely, may, can, will often, sometimes, often, almost, mostly, usually, generally, rarely, sometimes. Question writers insert these hedge phrases to cover every possibility. Often an answer choice will be wrong simply because it leaves no room for exception. Avoid answer choices that have definitive words like "exactly," and "always".

Switchback Words

Stay alert for "switchbacks". These are the words and phrases frequently used to alert you to shifts in thought. The most common switchback word is "but". Others include although, however, nevertheless, on the other hand, even though, while, in spite of, despite, regardless of.

New Information

Correct answer choices will rarely have completely new information included. Answer choices typically are straightforward reflections of the material asked about and will directly relate to the question. If a new piece of information is included in an answer choice that doesn't even seem to relate to the topic being asked about, then that answer choice is likely incorrect. All of the information needed to answer the question is usually provided for you, and so you should not have to make guesses that are unsupported or choose answer choices that require unknown information that cannot be reasoned on its own.

Time Management

On technical questions, don't get lost on the technical terms. Don't spend too much time on any one question. If you don't know what a term means, then since you don't have a dictionary, odds are you aren't going to get much further. You should immediately recognize terms as whether or not you know them. If you don't, work with the other clues that you have, the other answer choices and terms provided, but don't waste too much time trying to figure out a difficult term.

Contextual Clues

Look for contextual clues. An answer can be right but not correct. The contextual clues will help you find the answer that is most right and is correct. Understand the context in which a phrase or statement is made. This will help you make important distinctions.

Don't Panic

Panicking will not answer any questions for you. Therefore, it isn't helpful. When you first see the question, if your mind goes blank, take a deep breath. Force yourself to mechanically go through the steps of solving the problem and using the strategies you've learned.

Pace Yourself

Don't get clock fever. It's easy to be overwhelmed when you're looking at a page full of questions, your mind is full of random thoughts and feeling confused, and the clock is ticking down faster than you would like. Calm down and maintain the pace that you have set for yourself. As long as you are on track by monitoring your pace, you are guaranteed to have enough time for yourself. When you get to the last few minutes of the test, it may seem like you won't have enough time left, but if you only have as many questions as you should have left at that point, then you're right on track!

Answer Selection

The best way to pick an answer choice is to eliminate all of those that are wrong, until only one is left and confirm that is the correct answer. Sometimes though, an answer choice may immediately look right. Be careful! Take a second to make sure that the other choices are not equally obvious. Don't make a hasty mistake. There are only two times that you should stop before checking other answers. First is when you are positive that the answer choice you have selected is correct. Second is when time is almost out and you have to make a quick guess!

Check Your Work

Since you will probably not know every term listed and the answer to every question, it is important that you get credit for the ones that you do know. Don't miss any questions through careless mistakes. If at all possible, try to take a second to look back over your answer selection and make sure you've selected the correct answer choice and haven't made a costly careless mistake (such as marking an answer choice that you didn't mean to mark). This quick double check should more than pay for itself in caught mistakes for the time it costs.

Beware of Directly Quoted Answers

Sometimes an answer choice will repeat word for word a portion of the question or reference section. However, beware of such exact duplication – it may be a trap! More than likely, the correct choice will paraphrase or summarize a point, rather than being exactly the same wording.

Slang

Scientific sounding answers are better than slang ones. An answer choice that begins "To compare the outcomes…" is much more likely to be correct than one that begins "Because some people insisted…"

Extreme Statements

Avoid wild answers that throw out highly controversial ideas that are proclaimed as established fact. An answer choice that states the "process should be used in certain situations, if…" is much more likely to be correct than one that states the "process should be discontinued completely." The first is a calm rational statement and doesn't even make a definitive, uncompromising stance, using a hedge word "if" to provide wiggle room, whereas the second choice is a radical idea and far more extreme.

Answer Choice Families

When you have two or more answer choices that are direct opposites or parallels, one of them is usually the correct answer. For instance, if one answer choice states "x increases" and another answer choice states "x decreases" or "y increases," then those two or three answer choices are very similar in construction and fall into the same family of answer choices. A family of answer choices is when two or three answer choices are very similar in construction, and yet often have a directly opposite meaning. Usually the correct answer choice will be in that family of answer choices. The "odd man out" or answer choice that doesn't seem to fit the parallel construction of the other answer choices is more likely to be incorrect.

Special Report: How to Overcome Test Anxiety

The very nature of tests caters to some level of anxiety, nervousness or tension, just as we feel for any important event that occurs in our lives. A little bit of anxiety or nervousness can be a good thing. It helps us with motivation, and makes achievement just that much sweeter. However, too much anxiety can be a problem; especially if it hinders our ability to function and perform.

"Test anxiety," is the term that refers to the emotional reactions that some test-takers experience when faced with a test or exam. Having a fear of testing and exams is based upon a rational fear, since the test-taker's performance can shape the course of an academic career. Nevertheless, experiencing excessive fear of examinations will only interfere with the test-takers ability to perform, and his/her chances to be successful.

There are a large variety of causes that can contribute to the development and sensation of test anxiety. These include, but are not limited to lack of performance and worrying about issues surrounding the test.

Lack of Preparation

Lack of preparation can be identified by the following behaviors or situations:

Not scheduling enough time to study, and therefore cramming the night before the test or exam
Managing time poorly, to create the sensation that there is not enough time to do everything
Failing to organize the text information in advance, so that the study material consists of the entire text and not simply the pertinent information
Poor overall studying habits

Worrying, on the other hand, can be related to both the test taker, or many other factors around him/her that will be affected by the results of the test. These include worrying about:

Previous performances on similar exams, or exams in general
How friends and other students are achieving
The negative consequences that will result from a poor grade or failure

There are three primary elements to test anxiety. Physical components, which involve the same typical bodily reactions as those to acute anxiety (to be discussed below). Emotional factors have to do with fear or panic. Mental or cognitive issues concerning attention spans and memory abilities.

Physical Signals

There are many different symptoms of test anxiety, and these are not limited to mental and emotional strain. Frequently there are a range of physical signals that will let a test taker know that he/she is suffering from test anxiety. These bodily changes can include the following:

Perspiring
Sweaty palms
Wet, trembling hands
Nausea
Dry mouth
A knot in the stomach
Headache
Faintness
Muscle tension
Aching shoulders, back and neck
Rapid heart beat
Feeling too hot/cold

To recognize the sensation of test anxiety, a test-taker should monitor him/herself for the following sensations:

The physical distress symptoms as listed above
Emotional sensitivity, expressing emotional feelings such as the need to cry or laugh too much, or a sensation of anger or helplessness
A decreased ability to think, causing the test-taker to blank out or have racing thoughts that are hard to organize or control.

Though most students will feel some level of anxiety when faced with a test or exam, the majority can cope with that anxiety and maintain it at a manageable level. However, those who cannot are faced with a very real and very serious condition, which can and should be controlled for the immeasurable benefit of this sufferer.

Naturally, these sensations lead to negative results for the testing experience. The most common effects of test anxiety have to do with nervousness and mental blocking.

Nervousness

Nervousness can appear in several different levels:

The test-taker's difficulty, or even inability to read and understand the questions on the test
The difficulty or inability to organize thoughts to a coherent form
The difficulty or inability to recall key words and concepts relating to the testing questions (especially essays)
The receipt of poor grades on a test, though the test material was well known by the test taker

Conversely, a person may also experience mental blocking, which involves:

Blanking out on test questions
Only remembering the correct answers to the questions when the test has already finished.

Fortunately for test anxiety sufferers, beating these feelings, to a large degree, has to do with proper preparation. When a test taker has a feeling of preparedness, then anxiety will be dramatically lessened.

The first step to resolving anxiety issues is to distinguish which of the two types of anxiety are being suffered. If the anxiety is a direct result of a lack of preparation, this should be considered a normal reaction, and the anxiety level (as opposed to the test results) shouldn't be anything to worry about. However, if, when adequately prepared, the test-taker still panics, blanks out, or seems to overreact, this is not a fully rational reaction. While this can be considered normal too, there are many ways to combat and overcome these effects.

Remember that anxiety cannot be entirely eliminated, however, there are ways to minimize it, to make the anxiety easier to manage. Preparation is one of the best ways to minimize test anxiety. Therefore the following techniques are wise in order to best fight off any anxiety that may want to build.

To begin with, try to avoid cramming before a test, whenever it is possible. By trying to memorize an entire term's worth of information in one day, you'll be shocking your system, and not giving yourself a very good chance to absorb the information. This is an easy path to anxiety, so for those who suffer from test anxiety, cramming should not even be considered an option.

Instead of cramming, work throughout the semester to combine all of the material which is presented throughout the semester, and work on it gradually as the course goes by, making sure to master the main concepts first, leaving minor details for a week or so before the test.

To study for the upcoming exam, be sure to pose questions that may be on the examination, to gauge the ability to answer them by integrating the ideas from your texts, notes and lectures, as well as any supplementary readings.

If it is truly impossible to cover all of the information that was covered in that particular term, concentrate on the most important portions, that can be covered very well. Learn these concepts as best as possible, so that when the test comes, a goal can be made to use these concepts as presentations of your knowledge.

In addition to study habits, changes in attitude are critical to beating a struggle with test anxiety. In fact, an improvement of the perspective over the entire test-taking experience can actually help a test taker to enjoy studying and therefore improve the overall experience. Be certain not to overemphasize the significance of the grade - know that the result of the test is neither a reflection of self worth, nor is it a measure of intelligence; one grade will not predict a person's future success.

To improve an overall testing outlook, the following steps should be tried:

Keeping in mind that the most reasonable expectation for taking a test is to expect to try to demonstrate as much of what you know as you possibly can.
Reminding ourselves that a test is only one test; this is not the only one, and there will be others.
The thought of thinking of oneself in an irrational, all-or-nothing term should be avoided at all costs.
A reward should be designated for after the test, so there's something to look forward to. Whether it be going to a movie, going out to eat, or simply visiting friends, schedule it in advance, and do it no matter what result is expected on the exam.

Test-takers should also keep in mind that the basics are some of the most important things, even beyond anti-anxiety techniques and studying. Never neglect the basic social, emotional and biological needs, in order to try to absorb information. In order to best achieve, these three factors must be held as just as important as the studying itself.

Study Steps

Remember the following important steps for studying:

Maintain healthy nutrition and exercise habits. Continue both your recreational activities and social pass times. These both contribute to your physical and emotional well being.
Be certain to get a good amount of sleep, especially the night before the test, because when you're overtired you are not able to perform to the best of your best ability.
Keep the studying pace to a moderate level by taking breaks when they are needed, and varying the work whenever possible, to keep the mind fresh instead of getting bored. When enough studying has been done that all the material that can be learned has been learned, and the test taker is prepared for the test, stop studying and do something relaxing such as listening to music, watching a movie, or taking a warm bubble bath.

There are also many other techniques to minimize the uneasiness or apprehension that is experienced along with test anxiety before, during, or even after the examination. In fact, there are a great deal of things that can be done to stop anxiety from interfering with lifestyle and performance. Again, remember that anxiety will not be eliminated entirely, and it shouldn't be. Otherwise that "up" feeling for exams would not exist, and most of us depend on that sensation to perform better than usual. However, this anxiety has to be at a level that is manageable.

Of course, as we have just discussed, being prepared for the exam is half the battle right away. Attending all classes, finding out what knowledge will be expected on the exam, and knowing the exam schedules are easy steps to lowering anxiety. Keeping up with work will remove the need to cram, and efficient study habits will eliminate wasted time. Studying should be done in an ideal location for concentration, so that it is simple to become interested in the material and give it complete attention. A method such as SQ3R (Survey, Question, Read, Recite, Review) is a wonderful key to follow to make sure that the study habits are as effective as possible, especially in the case of learning from a textbook. Flashcards are great techniques for memorization. Learning to take good notes will mean that notes will be full of useful information, so that less sifting will need to be done to seek out what is pertinent for studying. Reviewing notes after class and then again on occasion will keep the information fresh in the mind. From notes that have been taken summary sheets and outlines can be made for simpler reviewing.

A study group can also be a very motivational and helpful place to study, as there will be a sharing of ideas, all of the minds can work together, to make sure that everyone understands, and the studying will be made more interesting because it will be a social occasion.

Basically, though, as long as the test-taker remains organized and self confident, with efficient study habits, less time will need to be spent studying, and higher grades will be achieved.

To become self confident, there are many useful steps. The first of these is "self talk." It has been shown through extensive research, that self-talk for students who suffer from test anxiety, should be well monitored, in order to make sure that it contributes to self confidence as opposed to sinking the student. Frequently the self talk of test-anxious students is negative or self-defeating, thinking that everyone else is smarter and faster, that they always mess up, and that if they don't do well, they'll fail the entire course. It is important to decreasing anxiety that awareness is made of self talk. Try writing any negative self thoughts and then disputing them with a positive statement instead. Begin self-encouragement as though it was a friend speaking. Repeat positive statements to help reprogram the mind to believing in successes instead of failures.

Helpful Techniques

Other extremely helpful techniques include:

Self-visualization of doing well and reaching goals
While aiming for an "A" level of understanding, don't try to "overprotect" by setting your expectations lower. This will only convince the mind to stop studying in order to meet the lower expectations.
Don't make comparisons with the results or habits of other students. These are individual factors, and different things work for different people, causing different results.
Strive to become an expert in learning what works well, and what can be done in order to improve. Consider collecting this data in a journal.
Create rewards for after studying instead of doing things before studying that will only turn into avoidance behaviors.
Make a practice of relaxing - by using methods such as progressive relaxation, self-hypnosis, guided imagery, etc - in order to make relaxation an automatic sensation.
Work on creating a state of relaxed concentration so that concentrating will take on the focus of the mind, so that none will be wasted on worrying.
Take good care of the physical self by eating well and getting enough sleep.
Plan in time for exercise and stick to this plan.

Beyond these techniques, there are other methods to be used before, during and after the test that will help the test-taker perform well in addition to overcoming anxiety.

Before the exam comes the academic preparation. This involves establishing a study schedule and beginning at least one week before the actual date of the test. By doing this, the anxiety of not having enough time to study for the test will be automatically eliminated. Moreover, this will make the studying a much more effective experience, ensuring that the learning will be an easier process. This relieves much undue pressure on the test-taker.

Summary sheets, note cards, and flash cards with the main concepts and examples of these main concepts should be prepared in advance of the actual studying time. A topic should never be eliminated from this process. By omitting a topic because it isn't expected to be on the test is only setting up the test-taker for anxiety should it actually appear on the exam. Utilize the course syllabus for laying out the topics that should be studied. Carefully go over the notes that were made in class, paying special attention to any of the issues that the professor took special care to emphasize while lecturing in class. In the textbooks, use the chapter review, or if possible, the chapter tests, to begin your review.

It may even be possible to ask the instructor what information will be covered on the exam, or what the format of the exam will be (for example, multiple choice, essay, free form, true-false). Additionally, see if it is possible to find out how many questions will be on the test. If a review sheet or sample test has been offered by the professor, make good use of it, above anything else, for the preparation for the test. Another great resource for getting to know the examination is reviewing tests from previous semesters. Use these tests to review, and aim to achieve a 100% score on each of the possible topics. With a few exceptions, the goal that you set for yourself is the highest one that you will reach.

Take all of the questions that were assigned as homework, and rework them to any other possible course material. The more problems reworked, the more skill and confidence will form as a result. When forming the solution to a problem, write out each of the steps. Don't simply do head work. By doing as many steps on paper as possible, much clarification and therefore confidence will be formed. Do this with as many homework problems as possible, before checking the answers. By checking the answer after each problem, a reinforcement will exist, that will not be on the exam. Study situations should be as exam-like as possible, to prime the test-taker's system for the experience. By waiting to check the answers at the end, a psychological advantage will be formed, to decrease the stress factor.

Another fantastic reason for not cramming is the avoidance of confusion in concepts, especially when it comes to mathematics. 8-10 hours of study will become one hundred percent more effective if it is spread out over a week or at least several days, instead of doing it all in one sitting. Recognize that the human brain requires time in order to assimilate new material, so frequent breaks and a span of study time over several days will be much more beneficial.

Additionally, don't study right up until the point of the exam. Studying should stop a minimum of one hour before the exam begins. This allows the brain to rest and put things in their proper order. This will also provide the time to become as relaxed as possible when going into the examination room. The test-taker will also have time to eat well and eat sensibly. Know that the brain needs food as much as the rest of the body. With enough food and enough sleep, as well as a relaxed attitude, the body and the mind are primed for success.

Avoid any anxious classmates who are talking about the exam. These students only spread anxiety, and are not worth sharing the anxious sentimentalities.

Before the test also involves creating a positive attitude, so mental preparation should also be a point of concentration. There are many keys to creating a positive attitude. Should fears become rushing in, make a visualization of taking the exam, doing well, and seeing an A written on the paper. Write out a list of affirmations that will bring a feeling of confidence, such as "I am doing well in my English class," "I studied well and know my material," "I enjoy this class." Even if the affirmations aren't believed at first, it sends a positive message to the subconscious which will result in an alteration of the overall belief system, which is the system that creates reality.

If a sensation of panic begins, work with the fear and imagine the very worst! Work through the entire scenario of not passing the test, failing the entire course, and dropping out of school, followed by not getting a job, and pushing a shopping cart through the dark alley where you'll live. This will place things into perspective! Then, practice deep breathing and create a visualization of the opposite situation - achieving an "A" on the exam, passing the entire course, receiving the degree at a graduation ceremony.

On the day of the test, there are many things to be done to ensure the best results, as well as the most calm outlook. The following stages are suggested in order to maximize test-taking potential:

Begin the examination day with a moderate breakfast, and avoid any coffee or beverages with caffeine if the test taker is prone to jitters. Even people who are used to managing caffeine can feel jittery or light-headed when it is taken on a test day.

Attempt to do something that is relaxing before the examination begins. As last minute cramming clouds the mastering of overall concepts, it is better to use this time to create a calming outlook.
Be certain to arrive at the test location well in advance, in order to provide time to select a location that is away from doors, windows and other distractions, as well as giving enough time to relax before the test begins.
Keep away from anxiety generating classmates who will upset the sensation of stability and relaxation that is being attempted before the exam.
Should the waiting period before the exam begins cause anxiety, create a self-distraction by reading a light magazine or something else that is relaxing and simple.

During the exam itself, read the entire exam from beginning to end, and find out how much time should be allotted to each individual problem. Once writing the exam, should more time be taken for a problem, it should be abandoned, in order to begin another problem. If there is time at the end, the unfinished problem can always be returned to and completed.
Read the instructions very carefully - twice - so that unpleasant surprises won't follow during or after the exam has ended.

When writing the exam, pretend that the situation is actually simply the completion of homework within a library, or at home. This will assist in forming a relaxed atmosphere, and will allow the brain extra focus for the complex thinking function.

Begin the exam with all of the questions with which the most confidence is felt. This will build the confidence level regarding the entire exam and will begin a quality momentum. This will also create encouragement for trying the problems where uncertainty resides.

Going with the "gut instinct" is always the way to go when solving a problem. Second guessing should be avoided at all costs. Have confidence in the ability to do well.

For essay questions, create an outline in advance that will keep the mind organized and make certain that all of the points are remembered. For multiple choice, read every answer, even if the correct one has been spotted - a better one may exist.

Continue at a pace that is reasonable and not rushed, in order to be able to work carefully. Provide enough time to go over the answers at the end, to check for small errors that can be corrected.

Should a feeling of panic begin, breathe deeply, and think of the feeling of the body releasing sand through its pores. Visualize a calm, peaceful place, and include all of the sights, sounds and sensations of this image. Continue the deep breathing, and take a few minutes to continue this with closed eyes. When all is well again, return to the test.

If a "blanking" occurs for a certain question, skip it and move on to the next question. There will be time to return to the other question later. Get everything done that can be done, first, to guarantee all the grades that can be compiled, and to build all of the confidence possible. Then return to the weaker questions to build the marks from there.

Remember, one's own reality can be created, so as long as the belief is there, success will follow. And remember: anxiety can happen later, right now, there's an exam to be written!

After the examination is complete, whether there is a feeling for a good grade or a bad grade, don't dwell on the exam, and be certain to follow through on the reward that was promised...and enjoy it! Don't dwell on any mistakes that have been made, as there is nothing that can be done at this point anyway.

Additionally, don't begin to study for the next test right away. Do something relaxing for a while, and let the mind relax and prepare itself to begin absorbing information again.

From the results of the exam - both the grade and the entire experience, be certain to learn from what has gone on. Perfect studying habits and work some more on confidence in order to make the next examination experience even better than the last one.
Learn to avoid places where openings occurred for laziness, procrastination and day dreaming.

Use the time between this exam and the next one to better learn to relax, even learning to relax on cue, so that any anxiety can be controlled during the next exam. Learn how to relax the body. Slouch in your chair if that helps. Tighten and then relax all of the different muscle groups, one group at a time, beginning with the feet and then working all the way up to the neck and face. This will ultimately relax the muscles more than they were to begin with. Learn how to breathe deeply and comfortably, and focus on this breathing going in and out as a relaxing thought. With every exhale, repeat the word "relax."

As common as test anxiety is, it is very possible to overcome it. Make yourself one of the test-takers who overcome this frustrating hindrance.

Special Report: Additional Bonus Material

Due to our efforts to try to keep this book to a manageable length, we've created a link that will give you access to all of your additional bonus material.

Please visit http://www.mometrix.com/bonus948/gacehistory to access the information.